THE DRILLING MACHINE

THE DRILLING MACHINE

IAN BRADLEY

MODEL & ALLIED PUBLICATIONS LTD.

Model & Allied Publications Ltd.
MAP Book Division
Station Road
Kings Langley
Hertfordshire

© Ian Bradley, 1973

First Published 1973

ISBN 0 852 42263 6

Printed in Great Britain by
Gilmour & Dean Ltd., Hamilton and London

CONTENTS

Servicing Parallel Shank Drills Servicing Taper Shank Drills

PREFACE

The Drilling Machine, even in its simplest form, is such an important item of equipment in the small workshop that it deserves more detailed written treatment than it normally receives.

For the most part, the owner of the small workshop is left to find out for himself, what can be done with a drilling machine and, sometimes painfully, what cannot.

In an attempt to gather together in one book as much relevant information as possible, the author addresses himself primarily to amateur workers and others whose requirements are covered by single spindle machines. It is hoped, however, that the professional production operative may find therein some crumbs of information that will prove useful to him.

Ian Bradley   *Hungerford, Berks., 1973*

CHAPTER ONE

HISTORICAL DERIVATIONS

It seems certain that, following the lathe, the drilling machine was one of the earliest tools to be developed from the primitive hand equipment at first available.

Of this what amounts to the carpenters brace appears to have been the first tool to have been adapted to machine form, however elementary. The adaption consisted of providing means of applying pressure to the brace in order to increase the facility of feeding the drill as well as measuring its rate of feed. In practical terms the work was supported on a simple stool while the brace itself was forced downward by a lever applied to its upper end. The elements of the device are depicted in the illustration *Fig. 1.1*. Naturally, such an arrangement was slow in operation, but it has survived in the drilling rigs sometimes used in railway track work.

The advent of the twist drill and, before it, the straight-flute drill, led to the production of geared hand braces capable of exploiting these drills more fully, and it was not long before the hand drills themselves were beginning to be mounted in fixtures enabling them to be used for the comparatively accurate drilling of work held in a vice or on the work table usually forming a part of the fitment. Some of the original work in this field came from the Millers Falls Co. of America, a typical example of their production being seen in the illustration *Fig. 1.2* which is taken from a tool merchants catalogue published in 1912.

The capacity of the hand brace used with the device was small and was, in fact, a maximum drill size of $\frac{3}{16}''$ dia. It became necessary, therefore, to provide machines, again based on the hand or more properly the breast drill, having a capacity of half an inch this being the maximum size of drill bit likely to be used in the light workshop. The equipment as illustrated in *Fig. 1.3* is an example derived from a half-inch capacity breast drill and made in the United States of America.

1

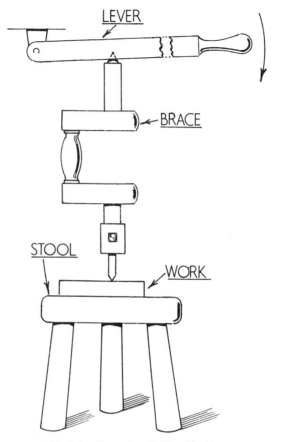

Fig. 1.1   Elementary Drilling Machine.

It must not be thought, however, that in England no progress was being made in this field. As far back as 1840 James Nasmyth of Steam Hammer fame, had produced a hand operated bench drill of a type still marketed as late as 1912 and perhaps later.

Nasmyth's machine is depicted in *Fig. 1.4* whilst its more modern counterpart is seen in the illustration *Fig. 1.5*.

At the time of the Great Exhibition of 1852 Joseph Whitworth had on show a collection of machine tools the range and quality of which were quite outstanding, and far surpassed anything his competitors could contrive.

Amongst them was the drilling machine illustrated in *Fig. 1.6*. This tool had embodied in it all the basic mechanical requirements expected today in a machine capable of drilling holes up to say $1\frac{1}{2}''$ dia. It had six spindle speeds. Three direct driven and three with back gear engaged. It also appears to have been provided with automatic feed to the drill spindle, though how this was driven is not clear, and a controlled rotatable work table mounted on a knee capable of rapid elevation by a hand wheel and a train of gears.

The turn of the century saw the flowering of amateur interest in workshop matters. The availability of small power prime movers such as the gas engine, and in some instances the steam engine, provided the users of the small workshop with ready means of relieving the human leg as a power producer. The wide-spread supply of electrical energy has, of course, extended the amateur's capability and has enabled him to invest in individually powered machines each fitted with its own electric motor. Early arrangements in this direction involved the adaption of drilling machines

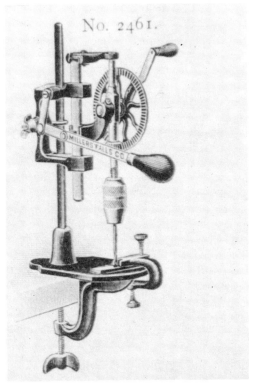

Fig. 1.2 Millers Falls Device.

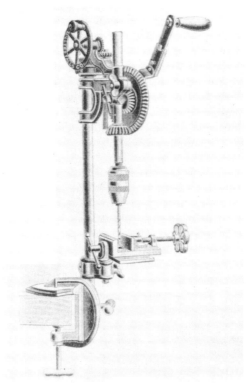

Fig. 1.3 $\frac{1}{2}''$ Capacity Drill in fixture.

originally intended for driving from a lineshaft, an independent electric motor being placed alongside the machine itself.

The 'Champion' Drilling Machine

One of the earlier machines available was the 'Champion' Drilling Machine, a later and more up to date version being illustrated in *Fig. 1.7*. This example differs little from the original design, except that it is larger with a capacity of $\frac{3}{8}$ inch instead of a $\frac{1}{4}$ inch as in the first models that were made. The machine illustrated has a belt guard and a simplified method of determining the depth to which the drill has penetrated.

There are two basic methods of carrying the drilling spindle. In the first, the spindle is carried directly in a pair of bearings with the driving pulley set on the shaft between them. In the second, the spindle is supported in a 'quill' passing through the lower part of the head casting, the spindle itself passing through the driving pulley that is set above the head casting. This pulley has a long sleeve extending into, and running in, the upper housing of the head casting. Both systems are illustrated diagrammatically in *Fig. 1.8*.

In both cases the pulleys have keys engaging keyways machined in the drill spindles themselves, these transmit the drive from the pulley to the spindle. One further very important design feature is the provision of bearings to take care of the thrust generated by the actual operation of drilling. The forces produced act, of course, in an upward direction so the thrust bearings are sited where these forces can best be absorbed. In the case of the arrangement seen at 'A' in the diagrammatic illustration this is at the top of the spindle where the feed lever makes contact, while at 'B' the thrust bearing is interposed between the bottom of the 'quill' and a face or shoulder on the lower part of the spindle itself.

The 'quill', its title will be apparent from reference to the feather of the goose, is a long cylinder, for the most part of cast iron, machined accurately both inside and out and having rack teeth cut

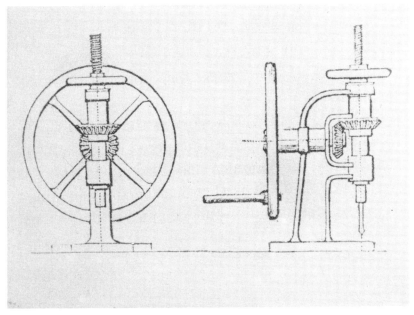

Fig. 1.4   Nasmyth's Bench Drill.

Fig. 1.5   Modern Nasmyth Drill.

upon it, or a rack attached to it so that a pinion fixed to the feed lever can mesh with the rack in order to afford vertical movement to any tool set in the drill chuck.

The arrangement as applied to the Champion Drilling Machine is depicted in the illustration *Fig. 1.9*, where the return spring arrangements for the quill are depicted in exploded form. The thrust bearing referred to earlier is sited at the bottom of the quill and may be seen in the previous illustration depicting the complete machine.

The 'Model Engineer' Drilling Machine

This highly successful machine, designed and developed by the late Edgar Westbury, is an example of the type of drill having the basic elements illustrated in *Fig. 1.8* at 'A'. It has the thrust bearing placed at the top of the spindle, this location serving also the anchorage for the feed lever which is pivoted through links on a lug forming part of the head casting. These details may be seen in *Fig. 1.10* and *Fig. 1.11*, where the complete head of the drilling machine with the feed lever and its counterpoise weight are illustrated.

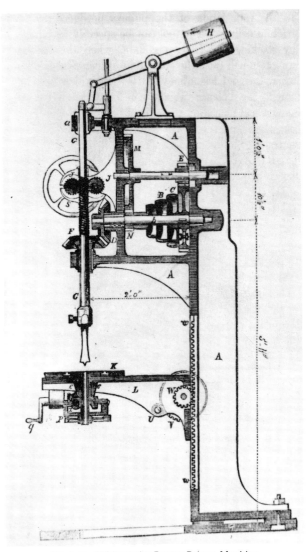

Fig. 1.6 Whitworths Power Driven Machine.

Fig. 1.7   The Champion Drilling Machine.

The Cowell Drilling Machines

The machines made by E. W. Cowell of Watford are designed to be made, or perhaps one should say completed, by the purchaser in his own workshop. To this end all the heavy machining that would be outside the resources of the amateur are carried out by the manufacturers in their own workshops, leaving the small work and light turning, together with the assembly of the completed machine, to its owner.

The Cowell Machines are made in two capacities, $\frac{3}{8}''$ and $\frac{1}{2}''$. Both have quill type spindles and both have their driving motors bolted to a mounting set behind the main column. The smaller of the two machines is seen in the illustration *Fig. 1.11*. The Cowell drilling machine has a fixed work table, so it cannot be tilted as can the table of the Champion drill for example, any angular drilling must therefore be carried out with the work secured in the appropriate fixtures mounted on the work table.

Medium Powered Drilling Machines

During the last war a number of medium powered drilling machines were imported from America. Their design was quite different from anything then made in England, based as it was on a tubular column supporting light section castings and the almost universal use of ball and roller bearings in a quill to carry the drill spindle itself. Many of these machines had back gear enabling quite large drills to be used.

Naturally, English design thinking was influenced by them and this led to the production of a number of drilling machines having all the American features but with possibly rather more robustness in general construction. Of this type of machine the author has owned two at one time or another.

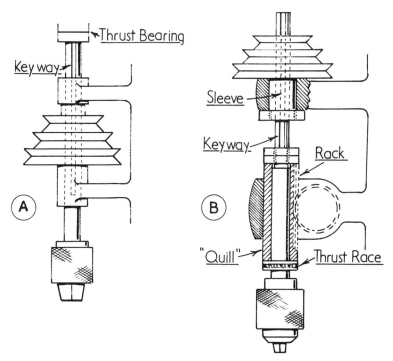

Fig. 1.8   Basic Elements of Drilling Machine design.

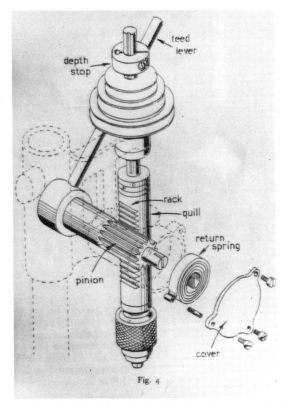

Fig. 1.9   The Champion Drilling Machine exploded view.

The Kerry Drilling Machine

The first American-type drilling machine in the author's possession was the Kerry, illustrated in *Fig. 1.12*. This had an open back gear sited at the top of the head casting and V-rope drive from the electric motor bolted to a platform behind the column. As will be seen it was a bench machine with a table that could be canted for angular drilling. Its maximum capacity was $\frac{3}{4}$ inch.

The Pacera Drilling Machine

Messrs. W. J. Meddings of Slough have done much to develop the American type of machine in this country. A typical example is seen in *Fig. 1.13*. It has back gear contained in an enclosed gearbox that can be filled with oil, and oil-gun lubrication through nipples to all points, such as the quill bearings, needing periodic lubrication.

A V-rope transmits power to the drill spindle and the multi-step pulleys fitted to the authors machine give the following drilling speeds.

Spindle Speeds R.P.M.

High	Low
310	80
500	130
1550	400
2770	700
4000	1000

From this it will be appreciated that the speed range available is sufficient for a very wide spectrum of drill sizes. The rack feed to the quill is sensitive so small drills, say down to $\frac{1}{16}''$ can be used in comfort. The work table may be tilted if need be, but the author

Fig. 1.10   M.E. Drill Thrust Assembly.

Fig. 1.11 The Cowell Drilling Machine $\frac{3}{8}''$ capacity.

prefers to retain it in the horizontal position that he has established with some accuracy.

Like the 'Kerry' drill previously mentioned the 'Pacera' machine may be obtained as a bench model but the example in the author's workshop is 'floor mounted' as have been others he has specified for various workshop duties elsewhere.

The Second-Hand Machine

So far we have considered drilling machines that will likely be bought new. It must not be forgotten, however, that second-hand machines come on the market from time to time, either at auction or as a private transaction, and that this may a source of supply favoured by many readers.

Elsewhere, notably in 'The Amateurs Workshop', the author has penned some notes on checking any machine offered for sale at second-hand; but it is felt that no manual devoted exclusively to the drilling machine could be considered complete without comprehensive reference to the subject, so the matter will be dealt with in the following chapter.

Modern Electric Hand Drills and Stands

The advent of 'Do-it-Yourself' has led to the development of electrically powered portable equipment designed to assist in woodwork and other operations needed around the house or elsewhere.

This equipment is, for the most part, based on the electric hand drills made by a number of specialist firms; these can be set in stands provided with lever operated carriages so forming a complete drilling machine.

Fig. 1.12   The Kerry Drilling Machine.

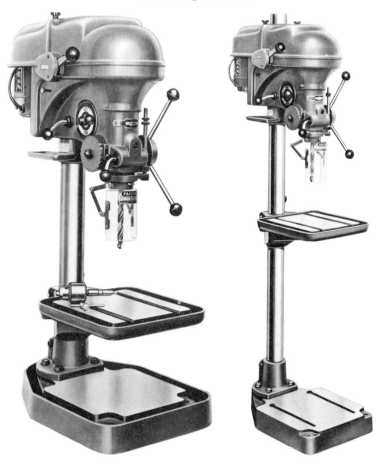

Fig. 1.13   The Pacera Drilling Machine.
Left: Bench Model   Right: Floor Model.

An example of this type of tool is illustrated in *Fig. 1.14* showing a Wolf electric hand drill and the stand made for it. It will be seen that it is possible to tilt the column so that angular drilling under controlled conditions may be undertaken. It seems fair to infer that the accent is on woodwork, though, of course, drilling in metal may be undertaken.

Some of the electric drills available have two speeds, as an example the $\frac{3}{8}''$ capacity Black and Decker machine used by the author has a low spindle speed of 900 r.p.m. and a top speed of 2600 r.p.m. These are speeds suited to small and medium sized drills.

Fig. 1.14   Wolf Drill on stand.

CHAPTER TWO

THE SECOND-HAND MACHINE

Unless he is conversant with certain basic features, the prospective purchaser of a second-hand drilling machine may well be in difficulty with an appraisal of its condition. A good superficial appearance is generally some guide as to quality; so, if the ability to drill holes without particular regard to accuracy will suffice, one may proceed to strike a bargain.

The machine that presents a battered look, and has its work table pock marked from having been used as a drilling bolster, had better be rejected at once as being unworthy of further consideration.

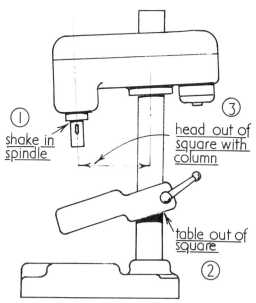

Fig. 2.1   Salient errors in a drilling machine.

16

For the most part, the would-be buyer expects his purchase to drill accurately. So, a few essential criteria need to be observed if the machine is to live up to his expectations.

In *Fig. 2.1* three salient errors in a drilling machine are depicted in an exaggerated form.

Testing the Machine

Shake in the drill spindle can be tested by the method illustrated in *Fig. 2.2*. A dial indicator with internal attachment mounted on a stand is set up on the work table. The finger of the attachment makes contact with the tapered bore of the spindle. Alternatively, if a chuck is permanently fitted, the spindle of the indicator contacts the shank of a drill set in the chuck. Side pressure applied to the drill will cause the drilling machine spindle to deflect the amount of the deflection being recorded by the dial indicator.

The set-up in the illustration may also be used to assess the accuracy of the tapered bore of the machine spindle, for it will be obvious that any error here will be reflected in the performance of the chuck itself.

The 'Turn Round' Test and other checks

If the work table is seriously out of square with the column of

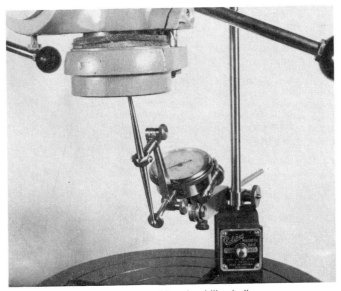

Fig. 2.2　Checking the drill spindle.

the drill no good work with the machine will be possible. A rough check, by unclamping the table and noting the amount of shake present, will determine the advisability of proceeding to further more critical examination. If there is no appreciable shake at this point an accurate square can be used to see if the work table surface is roughly at right angles to the drill column itself. The arrangement is depicted in the illustration *Fig. 2.3.*

If an out-of-square condition is observable its amount can be determined by means of a feeler gauge applied in the manner shown. An error of say 0.005″/0.010″ is tolerable in a machine intended for rough work only. Accurate drilling is only possible with a machine having a work table that is absolutely square with the machine column, a condition that can be tested in the following way.

A spindle is set in the chuck and on it is clamped the mounting for a dial test indicator having its foot applied to the surface of the work table itself. The end of the spindle, which is centre drilled, makes contact with a ball also set on the work table, the spindle itself being kept from rising by a weight attached to the machine's feed lever. After the indicator has been set at zero test readings are taken at the four stations marked 1, 2, 3 and 4 in the diagram *Fig. 2.4.* An equal reading of the test indicator at all four stations would indicate that the work table surface is at right angles to the column of the drilling machine. It is customary, however, to allow a plus

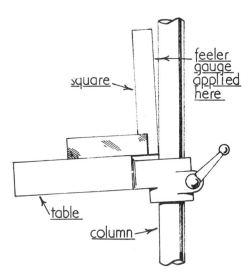

Fig. 2.3   Checking the squareness of the work table.

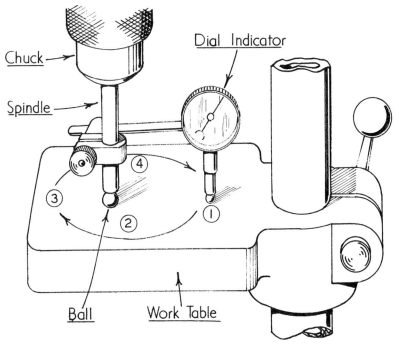

Fig. 2.4   The Turn Round Test.

reading of 0.001″ at station 3 in order to compensate for the load applied to the work table during the drilling operation.

The above test is, of course, dependent on the drill spindle and the column being parallel with one another. In a machine of proven quality one can assume that they will be so, because the process of boring the seatings for both the column and the spindle will have been carried out at a single setting. However, provided the test depicted in *Fig. 2.5*, shows no evidence of error, it is possible to make use of an accurate square to check the parallelism of the drill's column and spindle.

The method is to mount a dial indicator in the drill chuck and to apply its foot to the blade of the square set up on the work table as indicated in *Fig. 2.6*. The spindle itself may then be raised or lowered and readings taken from the dial indicator at the top and bottom of the blade of the square.

A better and more accurate method is to dispense with the square and cause the foot of the dial indicator to make contact with the column of the drilling machine itself. There can then be no doubt

Fig. 2.5   The Turn Round Test.

of the value of the test, since the check is directly between the spindle and the column. It should be noted that the indicator needs to be fitted with what is known as an 'elephant's foot'. Its name should be self-explanatory. It is used when the indicator is applied to round objects such as a drilling machine column or a thin edge like the blade of a square.

The second-hand machine should be examined for such matters as worn jockey pulleys, when these are fitted, and the spindles upon which the pulleys run. These are minor items of defect that an eventual purchaser may well be able to put right for himself. However, they may also provide a clue as to the general condition of the machine itself and so assist in an assessment of its true worth.

Electrical Equipment

It is always a difficult matter, when no apparatus is available, to make a check on any electrical gear that may be fitted to or offered with a second-hand machine. In any event it is really work for an experienced electrician so the most that can be done is to see that the driving motor is clean, that its bearings are not obviously worn and that, when started, it runs quietly. The general wiring should also be examined together with any switches that may be fitted.

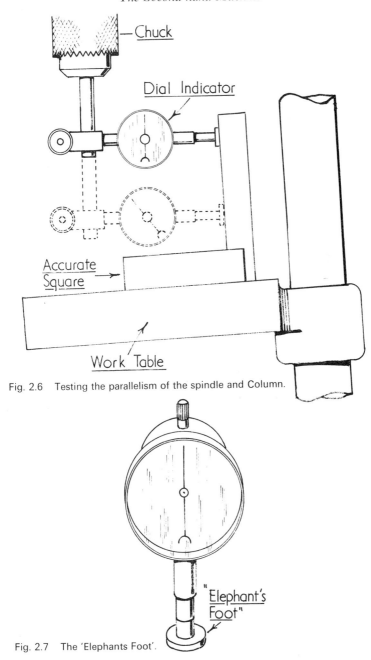

Fig. 2.6   Testing the parallelism of the spindle and Column.

Fig. 2.7   The 'Elephants Foot'.

CHAPTER THREE

INSTALLING AND DRIVING THE MACHINE

As we have seen, drilling machines suitable for use in the amateur and small workshop, while sometimes bolted directly to the floor, are for the most part, bench mounted.

The Machine Bench

So as in the main the amateurs machine tools are fastened to the bench in his workshop, we had best begin by discussing this very important piece of equipment. As the author has emphasised elsewhere, the bench must be really robust. Apart from the fact that the bench may also be used to mount a vice, and instability in this case would be most unfortunate, it is essential that the drilling machine, like other tools, is firmly mounted. It is foolish to make the bench from flimsy material. One pays good money for any machine tool these days so there is little point in perhaps spoiling

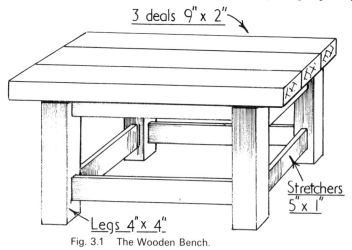

Fig. 3.1   The Wooden Bench.

its performance by mounting it inefficiently.

The type and size of bench used by the author is depicted in *Fig. 3.1*. The legs are made from oak which was freely available when the bench was made some 25 years ago. Today on cost alone the legs will likely have to be made from softer material. The bench illustrated is one half of the actual unit the author uses. This has six legs and is some 10 feet long. Heavy stretchers are employed, one set placed directly under the bench top, the other set low down on the legs. These last serving as supports for boxes containing heavy material that act as ballast for the bench and its contents.

Driving Bench Mounted Machines

For the most part the amateur's drilling machine is a simple tool having its driving motor quite independently mounted. There are then three ways of locating the motor, these are:—

1) On the bench behind the drilling machine.
2) Under the bench.
3) Under the machine which is itself bolted to a base plate standing on the bench top.

The three sitings are depicted in the illustration *Fig. 3.2*.

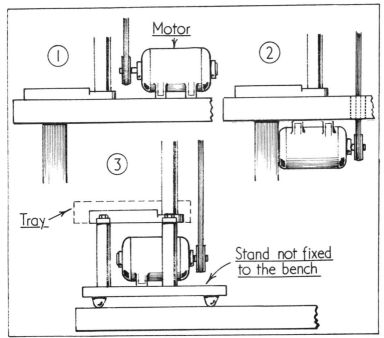

Fig. 3.2   Three sitings for the Drilling Machine Motor.

Of the fixed bench positions No. 2 is probably the most suitable. Placed under the bench top the motor is of course protected from the swarf which will inevitably be present during the drilling operation; moreover the motor now takes up no valuable space on the bench top.

The arrangement depicted at (3) may appeal to those who need a self-contained unit that may be carried around and used wherever convenient. The author has a small $\frac{1}{4}''$ 'Champion' drilling machine fitted up in this way.

It will be noticed that in all three set-ups the base of the drilling machine is brought well forward to the front of the bench. The reason for this should be obvious. Some workers prefer to have a tray round the machine to catch any swarf that is made. With the motor mounted as in position (3) a tray is essential. In the authors

Fig. 3.3   Motor mounting with belt tensioning device.

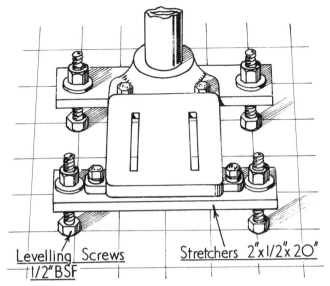

Levelling Screws   Stretchers 2″x 1/2″x 20″
1/2″ BSF

Fig. 3.4   Floor mounting with levelling screws.

case the tray, indicated by the dotted lines, is interposed between the base of the drill and the top of the uprights that support it.

The motor position now finding general approval is that illustrated in *Fig. 3.3*. Here the motor is mounted directly behind the head of the drilling machine on a special platform provided with a cam operated belt-tensioning device. This device enables the belt to be quickly slackened when it needs to be moved from one step on the driving pulley to another, and tightened afterwards.

It is perhaps worth noting that motors to be used in this location must be so designed that their bearings can accept end loading, otherwise undue wear will quickly take place.

Make sure that any machines placed on the bench are well secured. For the smaller drills woodscrews will suffice but coach bolts will be needed for any heavier machines.

Floor Mounted Machines

The type of floor mounted drill which is simply a column extension of a bench machine needs to be secured firmly since the base area of this class of tool is not large.

However, if the permanent fixture of the drill is likely to be an embarrassment, one may extend the footing in the manner depicted in the illustration *Fig. 3.4*.

Such an arrangement provides a firm support for the machine and enables it to be set level by means of the screws threaded into the stretchers. These can be locked by nuts once the levelling operation has been completed.

In the case of the permanently fixed machine, whether on the bench or on the floor, it is also important to see that it is level when bolted down. A spirit level set on the base plate, not on the work table for this may have been disturbed, will allow the levelling to be checked. It is by no means certain that the floor of every amateur's workshop is fit for the immediate setting down of any machine. If, as was the situation in one of the authors workshops, the floor consists of soft brick, worn by the passage of countless feet (the place was once the village shop) the only recourse is to remove the bricks, dig out an area about 9″ to one foot deep and some 6″ wider than the base of the machine itself, then fill in with concrete and trowel as flat and level as possible. By making a template of the base plate and setting it in place with the necessary bolts in it one can grout them in at the same time as laying the foundation for the drill.

Some readers may have premises that lend themselves to the installation of lineshafting. Where this is possible there may be many advantages for the amateur who is considering a gradual increase in the facilities of his workshop. Once the lineshafting and its bearings have been assembled and erected, with an electric motor or other source of power sited at some convenient point, one has a choice of location for any machine tool. Moreover, with pulleys

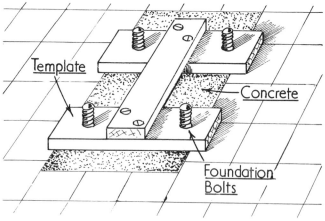

Fig. 3.5   Template for Foundation Bolts.

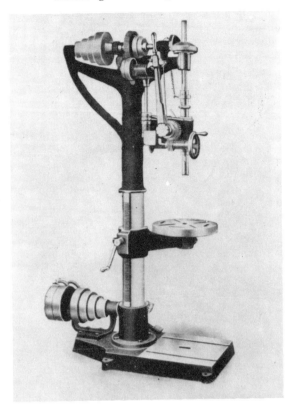

Fig. 3.6   Heavy Drilling Machine.

available that may be detached and replaced without disturbing the lineshafting itself, the location of machines may be changed if required.

For those who need a heavy drilling machine of the type illustrated in *Fig. 3.6* a drive from lineshafting, while not essential, is the most convenient method. Drills of this pattern for the most part, have their own countershaft set on the baseplate itself. This can be driven directly from the lineshafting, a flat belt, of course, being used.

Belts and Belting

The driving belts for the drilling machine take three forms:—
1) Round belts for the smaller machine.
2) V-ropes for the self-contained motor driven machine.

3) Flat belting for the driving of the older pattern drilling machine.

Round belting is usually made from leather, though it is possible to obtain endless rubber-and-canvas belts of a fair length range. For the most part the amateur will rely on the leather belt to drive his machines. Some samples obtainable are not good but belting sold by sewing machine shops, when they stock it, always appears to be of high quality.

Fasteners for round belting commonly take the form illustrated in *Fig. 3.7* at 'A'. The fastener is a short length of piano wire, about 18–20 standard wire gauge, passed through a hole in each end of the belt and clinched over as depicted.

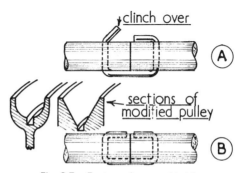

Fig. 3.7   Fastener for round belting.

If left in this condition, and run over small pulleys at a high speed, the fastener will tend to be productive of unwanted noise. However, by sinking the fastener into the belt, as indicated at 'B' in *Fig. 3.7*, and combining this procedure with the turning of a groove in any pulleys the belt may run over, noise may be largely reduced if not wholly eliminated. Complete elimination of noise, if required, can be obtained by scarfing the ends of the belt and cementing them together with a cellulose cement such as Durofix. The scarfing can be performed with a small plane with the belt resting on a wooden board, but the cementing needs a small fixture if it is to be carried out satisfactorily.

The two stages in the making of the joint are depicted in *Fig. 3.8* at 'A' and 'B'. If additional strength is needed then the joint can be sewn in the manner illustrated at 'C' AFTER the cement has set. The sewing is best carried out with waxed thread through drilled holes evenly spaced along the joint. A single pass of thread will usually suffice with the ends of the thread secured by belt cement.

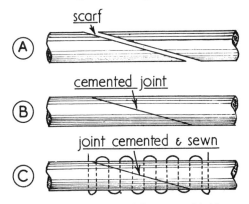

Fig. 3.8   Cemented and Sewn round belting.

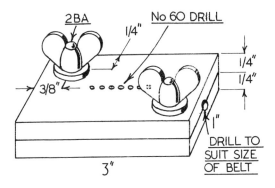

Fig. 3.9   Jig for cementing a round belt.

Additional strength may be obtained by doubling the sewing. When making the joint the thread is, of course, drawn tight.

The smallest belt that can be treated is one of $\frac{1}{4}''$ diameter.

A Belt Cementing Fixture

The fixture that has been referred to consists of two mild steel plates held together by a pair of studs and wing nuts, and drilled axially as depicted to accept the belt to be cemented. The fixture also acts as a jig for drilling the holes needed when sewing the belt.

The parts of the device are illustrated in *Fig. 3.11* together with a fixture made for the purpose of cutting the scarf on the belt itself. The parts of this fixture illustrated at (1) and (2) comprise a steel block drilled at an angle to allow the belt to be passed through and

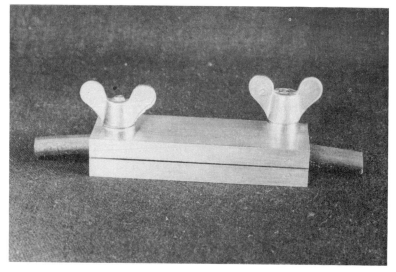

Fig. 3.10   The Jig.

Fig. 3.11   The Jig opened with scarfing device.

a sliding mount for the razor blade used to shave the belt. A small hole in the side of the block is provided so that, after drilling, a pin can be passed through the belt to hold it during the shaving operation.

This fixture is reasonably successful but it has been found that it is better to use a small carpenter's plane for the purpose since the operation can be better controlled by this means. Two pieces of wood are then clamped each side of the block with their edges just clear of the block so that the blade of the plane is protected.

Flat Belting

Flat belting is obtainable in leather, in rubber-and-canvas and in cotton; the last being impregnated with latex to increase the gripping power of the belt and inhibit its attraction to damp. Leather, though generally the most expensive, is in the end the most economical belt material for use in the amateur workshop, and belts made from it are very flexible and have a long working life. There are, of course, several proprietary belt fasteners on the market, and readers may be content to make use of one of these; the author, however, has for many years made use of two simple methods of belt fastening for flat leather belting. The first of these has already been described when discussing the jointing of round belts. The cemented joint is a very satisfactory way of jointing a flat leather belt, it is easy to make and will last a long time, 20 years in the case of one belt in the author's workshop.

A well-made belt joint has great durability. Its edges need to be cut dead square and they have to be butted firmly. This condition can be secured by sewing the joint in the manner illustrated in *Fig. 3.12.* Copper wire, some 22 or 24 standard wire gauge, is used and is threaded through drilled holes in the ends of the belt according to the pattern shown in the illustration. On the underside of the belt

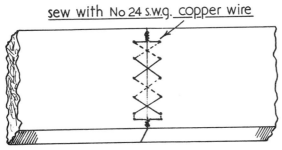

Fig. 3.12   Sewing a leather belt.

the wire must be sunk below the surface. This is brought about by the cutting of shallow grooves with a sharp chisel in the leather itself. In this way the wire cannot come into contact with the pulleys over which the belt will eventually run.

V-ropes

The modern self-contained drilling machine is fitted with an endless V-rope, a form of rubber-canvas belting, having considerable gripping power. V-ropes for the most part have the maker's name, a reference number and often a figure denoting length. So when a replacement is needed the user has all the information required to obtain it. Unless any V-ropes in use are made from Neoprene rubber care must be taken to see that they do not come into contact with oil or they will soon be ruined. Fortunately, the belt layout of the drilling machine makes this eventuality unlikely.

Electrical Installation

The motors used in the small workshop are, for the most part, of low power and under a 1 h.p. rating. Providing the machines to be installed all have their own switches fitted, they may be fed from plugs and sockets placed strategically below the bench. These can be supplied with current through a Double-Pole switch and fuses located on the leg of the bench. In this way the whole bench electrical system can be isolated when required. The author prefers this method; the wiring up to the sockets is work for a qualified electrician, a status few amateurs possess. So it is advisable to let the expert carry out any wiring installation up to the sockets. If fused 13 amp plugs are used connections can be made by the amateur himself as any wrong connections made will only result in a blown local fuse. However, should there be any doubt as to the right way to make the necessary connections to a machine the qualified man should be consulted.

Lighting the Work Table

It cannot be gainsaid that adequate lighting directed on the work table is essential. In industrial circles it has long been recognised that work mounted in any machine tool must be well lit, and the drilling machine is no exception to this requirement.

Many American-made drills have long had built-in lighting focussed on the work table, but it seems to have been slow in gaining a foothold on machines designed for amateur use in this country.

One may fill this lack of illumination for oneself, however, as the two illustrations *Fig. 3.13* and *Fig. 3.14* will confirm. This fitment was contrived from a lamp holder and reflector that once formed part of the lighting fitted in the navigators compartment of military aircraft. The lamp mounting is a split ring that is spring loaded so that it is a friction fit round the column of the drilling machine. It is readily moveable but will stay firm wherever it is put. In the illustration the attachment is seen fitted to the column of one of the older type of Cowell Bench drills.

The lamp holder itself will accept small bayonet cap lamps. Those readers, like the author, who have a low-voltage electric system in their workshops will find this convenient when using any double-pole aircraft or car lamp bulbs that may be available; on

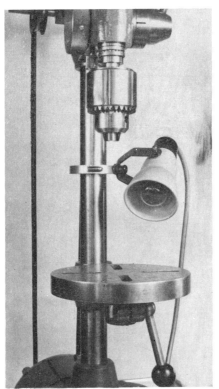

Fig. 3.13   Drilling Machine Lamp attachment.

the other hand there is available a 240–250 volt, 15 watt lamp, and this has, in practice, been found to give adequate lighting to the work table.

Fig. 3.14   Parts of the attachment.

CHAPTER FOUR

DRILLS AND DRILL CHUCKS

The drills originally in use were of the type illustrated in *Fig. 4.1*. These were known as spear point drills and were employed for both metal and wood. They were readily knocked up by the blacksmith who was, presumably, their principal user. The drilling machine depicted in the illustration *Fig. 4.2* has a spear point drill

Fig. 4.1   The Spear Point Drill.

Fig. 4.2   Drilling Machine with Spear Point Drill.

35

set in the spindle. The drill itself is one of a pair of machine tools used in the building of the original Crystal Palace. The other is a combined guillotine-and-punch employed in cutting off lengths of material for use in the construction of the Palace. As to the drilling machine itself, the treadle operated feed for the drill spindle is of interest because, as may be seen, it left both the operator's hands free to direct the work. Illustrations and descriptions of tools published about 1850 show that the spear point drill was still in regular use then and it must have remained so till the straight-flute drill depicted in *Fig. 4.3* was introduced. This drill came from America and was the product of the famous Samuel Morse who gave his name to many innovations and founded an organisation devoted, for the most part, to the production of drilling equipment.

Fig. 4.3   The Straight Flute Drill.

The straight-flute drill was an ideal tool for use on brass as it would not 'grab', either when actually drilling or when breaking through on completing the hole, and it is said that the late Sir Henry Royce used to insist on the employment of straight-flute drills for certain work. When used on steel the straight-flute drill did not have the free cutting power for which industry was seeking. A little consideration will show the reader that the reason for this deficiency is the lack of top rake possessed by the drill's cutting edge, hence its effectiveness on brass.

The introduction of the spiral-fluted twist drill having plenty of top-rake provided industry with the tool it needed and led to the gradual phasing out of the straight-fluted drill until today it is virtually unobtainable.

The Twist Drill

Twist drills may be obtained in several forms having three spiral pitches as depicted in the illustration *Fig. 4.4*. The most common form are called 'jobbers drills'; they have a normal spiral and, for the most part, a fluted portion some two-thirds the length of the drill as a whole.

Jobbers drills are not always suitable. The hole to be drilled may be so deep that this form of drill is too short to be of service. It is then that the workman will have to recourse to a 'long series' drill. Usually these drills are about twice as long as a jobbers drill, but

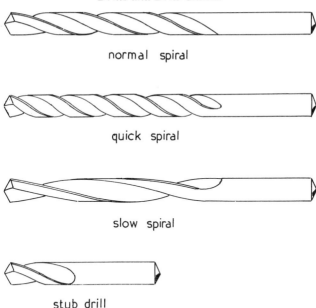

normal spiral

quick spiral

slow spiral

stub drill

Fig. 4.4   Twist Drills.

they may be obtained in a variety of lengths as the following examples stocked in the author's workshop will demonstrate:—

Inch Fractional	*Number*
$1/16'' \times 6''$ long	No. $12 \times 8''$ long
$3/32'' \times 6''$ long	$14 \times 6\frac{1}{2}''$ long
$5/32'' \times 10''$ long	$30 \times 6\frac{1}{2}''$ long
$3/16'' \times 7\frac{1}{2}''$ long	
$11/64'' \times 10''$ long	
$15/64'' \times 9''$ long	

Do not expect to be able to buy 'long series' drills at the local iron-mongers; toolmerchants of some standing should be able to obtain them, however.

For the most part drills having a normal spiral are those most commonly used. However, for certain purposes the two alternative spirals illustrated are sometimes employed. Quick spiral drills, because of their increased top rake, cut light alloy readily, while slow spiral drills are useful in the drilling of plastic material. The amateur worker, however. will usually employ drills having a normal spiral unless, for any reason, he finds specialist equipment really necessary.

The Stub Drill

The fourth drill illustrated in *Fig. 4.4* is the stub drill. This tool, for the most part, is approximately one-third the length of a jobbers drill. Consequently size-for-size, a stub drill is the more rigid of the two and so very suitable for use in hand drills or in a machine when a number of holes of similar size have to be drilled. The rigidity of the stub drill makes the starting of these holes much easier. Stub drills are also of use in a machine when the distance between the work and the drill is much restricted.

Extension Drills

In an emergency a substitute for a long series drill can be contrived by grafting a standard jobbers drill on to a piece of silver steel. The combination is suitable for use when the hole to be drilled cannot be reached by normal length drill and when the depth of the hole is small.

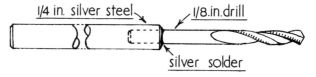

Fig. 4.5   The Extension Drill. Small sizes.

A typical extension drill is depicted in the illustration *Fig. 4.5*. A length of $\frac{1}{4}''$ silver is drilled axially and an $\frac{1}{8}''$ diameter twist drill is silver soldered to it as shown in the illustration. The drill must be made a firm fit in the axial hole, or it will not run true. To this end it pays to make the hole in the steel extension slightly smaller than the shank of the drill which can be polished down by stoning until the drill is a firm fit in the hole. This practice will ensure that the drill point runs truly, always provided of course that the hole itself has been drilled concentrically in the first place.

Extensions to large drills, say from $\frac{3}{8}''$ and upwards, can be made in the manner depicted in *Fig. 4.6*. The procedure is much the same as that previously described, but in this instance the extension is the same diameter as that of the drill itself.

TURN DOWN TO FIT

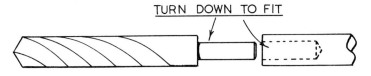

BRAZE

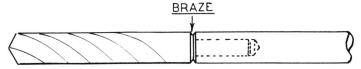

Fig. 4.6   The Extension Drill. Large sizes.

Fig. 4.7   The Slocombe Centre Drill.

It should, perhaps, be pointed out that drill shanks are, commonly, soft enough to allow them to be turned down to size.

The Centre Drill

The drill depicted in *Fig. 4.7*, is a specially designed tool for picking up centres on marked-out work so that it can be drilled correctly. The centre drill is in reality a combination consisting of a small pilot drill for picking up purposes and a larger countersunk drill that acts as a pilot for starting the main drill. Centre drills are available in the following sizes:—

Size	Body dia. in.	Drill Point dia. in.
B.S.1	1/8	3/64
B.S.2	3/16	1/16
B.S.3	1/4	3/32
B.S.4	5/16	1/8
B.S.5	7/16	3/16
B.S.6	5/8	1/4
B.S.7	3/4	5/16

Morse Taper Shanks

We have already dealt with drills having parallel shanks designed for use in chucks, themselves secured to the drilling machine spindle. There is a second class, however, that may be directly mounted in the drill spindle. These have tapered shanks machined to a standard known as the Morse Taper. There are five sizes of this standard numbered from 1–5, but of these the amateur, for the most part, will only be interested in the two smaller sizes that is No. 1 and No. 2 Morse Taper.

Drills having tapered shanks are provided with a tang at their upper end. This has a double purpose. Firstly, to take the drive from the drill spindle and prevent any slip between the shank and the spindle; secondly, to allow the use of a drift to extract the drill from the spindle. These points are illustrated in *Fig. 4.8*.

Fig. 4.8   Drills with Morse Taper Shanks.

It will be clear that the running accuracy of a taper shank drill is very dependent on the surface condition of the taper itself. If, therefore, any of these drills are to be bought at second-hand they should be examined for bruising on the shank and rejected if the bruising is severe. Mild bruising, however, can usually be polished away with a dead smooth file leaving the drill perfectly serviceable. These matters are also dealt with in 'The Amateurs Workshop' published by Model and Allied Press Ltd.

Drill Sizes

There are several categories of twist drill. The first of these is the inch fractional category. This covers drills in increments of $\frac{1}{64}$ " to 1 inch and over starting at $\frac{1}{32}$ ". There is then the category covering the number size drills. Number drills start at No. 80 (0.0138" dia.) and finish at No. 0 (.2280"). The increments here are variable. At the lower end of the list the increments are a few ten-thousandths of an inch while at the top they may vary as much as 0.008".

Letter Size drills start where the Number drills leave off. So letter A is 0.234" dia. the range extending to letter Z (0.413" dia.). Here the increments vary from about 0.004" at the commencement of the list to some 0.010" at the end of it.

For some time now a range of drills based on metric measurements has been available. Their range may be examined in the list of Twist Drills to be found at the end of this book. Metric drills in small sizes at all events provide the user with drills, if employed with the ranges already described, that will enable him to cover a wide spectrum of diameters by very close increments, and there seems little doubt that, in time, and by the addition of more sizes, metric drills will make both Letter and Number sizes redundant.

Drill Materials

For the most part twist drills are made either from carbon steel or high-speed steel. In the past the small workshop user has tended to use drills made from carbon steel, possible because they were cheaper; but the superior performance of the high-speed variety

Fig. 4.9   The Jacobs Chuck.

seems to be convincing many, and not necessarily with a commercial background either, that their ability to be run at almost twice the speed of a carbon steel drill, coupled with their increased length of cutting life between re-grinds, makes the extra cost well worth while if only for a few selected sizes and applications.

Drill Chucks

At one time there was a number of different types of chuck on the market. These varied both in their ability to hold drills firmly and in the accuracy of their running. Many of the designs have not stood the test of time so, though interesting as museum pieces, are not worth further consideration.

One design, however, has become pre-eminent largely because, as a piece of engineering, it is both simple and correct; whilst the workmanship put into it is an outstanding example of accurate quantity production. The chuck in question is the Jacobs chuck now made in many sizes. The chuck itself is illustrated in *Fig. 4.9* where it will be seen that two standard mountings are available.

That most commonly employed is the tapered mount secured

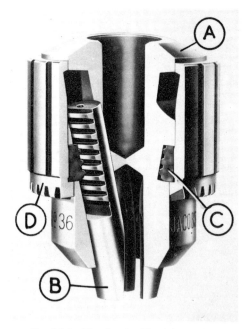

Fig. 4.10   The Jacobs Chuck in section.

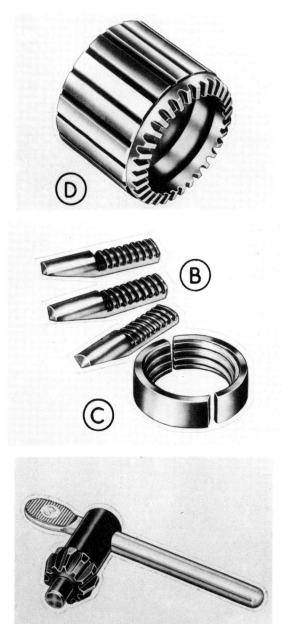

Fig. 4.11   Parts of the Jacobs Chuck.

directly to the machine spindle by friction only. An alternative, used when the machine spindle is bored to a standard Morse Taper, is to set the chuck on a tapered arbor which itself fits within the machine spindle.

Jacobs chucks are also available with a thread mounting, a method normally employed with portable tools.

The chuck has but a few working parts illustrated in *Fig. 4.11*. These comprise the Body 'A', three Jaws 'B', the nut 'C' and the sleeve 'D'. The jaws are set in the Body at an angle and are fed forward by the nut which is a press fit in the sleeve. The sleeve can be turned by hand to set a drill in place but, unless the drill is small hand pressure is insufficient to secure it. A Key with a small pinion machined on its shank is therefore provided to engage the sleeve and turn the nut with sufficient force to ensure that the drill is firmly gripped.

The range of available Jacobs chucks is wide and comprises medium duty, heavy duty and extra heavy duty units. These last have a ball thrust race incorporated with the nut allowing greatly increased gripping power to be exerted on the drill itself.

All Jacobs chucks have a nominal minimum holding capacity of zero and will hold a No. 70 drill. The smallest chuck in the range with a maximum capacity of $\frac{5}{32}''$ is capable of holding a No. 80 drill accurately.

Keyless Chucks—The 'Albrecht'

In the past several makes of keyless drill chucks have been available, many of them of doubtful quality. However, the 'Albrecht' chuck illustrated in *Fig. 4.12* is not amongst this low-class equip-

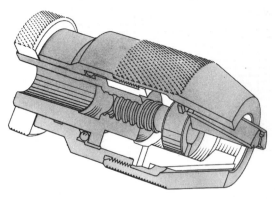

Fig. 4.12   The 'Albrecht' Chuck in section.

ment for it is a device of the highest standard. Its gripping power is very great and it is capable of holding small drills firmly and without damage.

Those workers who have to use drills of very small diameter will be interested in the 'Albrecht' chuck depicted in *Fig. 4.13*. The mounting of very small drills in a chuck is usually attended by the difficulty of centering them within its jaws. As will be seen in the illustration the smallest chuck in the 'Albrecht' range has an engraved index ring enabling the user to set the chuck jaws so that the drill to be mounted will slide into place directly and not wander away from the gripping faces as might otherwise occur.

Fig. 4.13   The small 'Albrecht' Chuck.

Securing the Drill Chuck

When fitting the chuck to a tapered arbor or directly to the spindle all traces of grease or oil must be removed from the mating faces by washing them with Triclorethylene. The chuck can then be put in place and given a smart tap with a raw hide mallet. This treatment will usually suffice to secure the chuck. However, for those who feel that additional security is desirable, the procedure illustrated in *Fig. 4.14* can be recommended. The illustration is perhaps self-explanatory. The sizes shown for the screw holding the chuck in place and for the tapped hole to accept a jacking screw for removal purposes, are suitable for use with the smallest size of Jacobs chuck.

A word of warning however. Care should be taken to see that the design of the chuck is such that the fitting of an axial screw will not harm it. If adopted in conjunction with the 'Albrecht' chuck, already sectioned in *Fig. 4.12*, the results would be fatal.

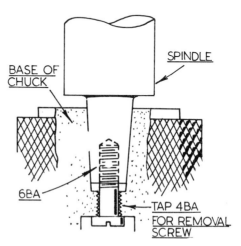

Fig. 4.14   Method of securing a drill chuck.

CHAPTER FIVE

SERVICING THE DRILLING EQUIPMENT

If we except adequate maintainance of the drilling machine itself, servicing the drilling equipment consists in seeing that the drills to be used are sharp. This involves an understanding of the factors governing the drill point and the angles to which it needs to be ground in order to obtain the best results. The diagram *Fig. 5.1,*

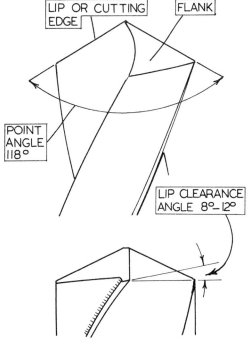

Fig. 5.1   The Drill Point.

47

depicts these angles and also gives the names usually applied to the parts of the drill point.

The first and perhaps most important angle is that imparted, during the grinding process, to the point itself. For general purposes this angle is, for the most part, set at 118°. Next, and in order that the drill shall cut at all, the flank behind the tip or cutting edge needs a clearance of from 8°–12°. It is of the utmost importance that after grinding the drill point shall be symmetrical. If not and for example, one lip is longer than the other then the drilled hole will be oversize. By the same token a reduction of lip clearance below that given will cause the drill to cut in a sluggish manner, while an increased clearance is most likely to result in a break up of the lip itself.

The Grinding Machine

If the drills are to be ground correctly it is essential that the grinding equipment should be above reproach. At one time it was possible to purchase grinding heads, albeit with plain bearings, that did excellently for the purpose of drill and tool grinding. Today, however, simple but good grinding heads do not appear available. In the past designs for simple but practical equipment have appeared in the press, and may yet again in the future, so it is still possible for the amateur worker to make a grinding head for himself. For those who do not wish to do so, or cannot spare the time for the work, several makes of electric grinder are purchaseable all of course well fitted for the purpose intended. These machines will have the grinding wheels correctly mounted. But for those who are not aware of the necessary conditions that govern a properly secured wheel, these are set out diagrammatically in the illustration *Fig. 5.2.* The fixed flange, abutting a shoulder on the spindle, is usually secured against rotation by a key, whilst the loose flange, perhaps as its name implies, is not secured against rotation though it is free to slide on the spindle itself. A little consideration will show that the fixed flange must run truly or the grinding wheel will wobble when set in place. If a second-hand machine is under consideration this is a point that should be watched and, if confirmed, its rectification allowed for.

The flanges must never be allowed to bear directly on the grinding wheels. Instead paper or card washers need to be placed between the flanges and the wheel, these will bed the wheel securely.

Grinding Wheel Speeds

It is important that the wheels are run at the correct speed or the grinding carried out will be unefficient. If the best results are to be

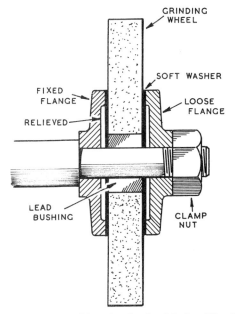

Fig 5.2   Correct Mounting for the Grinding Wheel.

realised grinding wheels should be driven at an approximate surface speed of some 5,000 ft. per minute. Based on this figure the following table gives the spindle speed required for the most commonly employed wheel sizes:—

Wheel Diameter	Wheel revs. per minute
3	6,400
4	4,800
5	3,800
6	3,200

Producers of commercially made electrically driven grinding machines will see to it that these requirements are met, and those who may be considering making their own equipment would do well to adhere to them.

Dressing the Grinding Wheel

When first set in place, and at regular intervals thereafter, it is necessary to true the surface of the grinding wheel, by applying to it a dresser especially designed for the purpose. The dresser, for the most part, may take two forms. Either it is an industrial diamond set in a holder so that it may be brought to bear on the wheel, or it is a combination of star wheels and discs mounted on a spindle for the same purpose. Their action on the wheel is to break up the bond which holds the wheels together and so to bring to the surface fresh sharp abrasive grains in place of those blunted by the grinding process itself. The matter is dealt with more comprehensively than is possible here in 'Sharpening Small Tools' by 'Duplex' and published by Model & Associated Press Ltd.

The dressing operation is attended by the production of much abrasive dust, so the grinding machine should, if possible, be located well away from machine tools.

Grinding the Twist Drill

There are two ways to grind a twist drill. The first way is to sharpen it freehand, while the second, and more accurate method, makes use of a jig or fixture attached to the grinding machine that will control the movement of the drill point in relation to the wheel and so impart the necessary point and clearance angles referred to earlier.

However, it is not everyone who has access to a twist drill grinding jig, recourse therefore must be had to the freehand, sometimes called offhand, methods.

Freehand Grinding

The series of diagrams comprising the illustration *Fig. 5.3* depict, so far as is possible, the procedure and checks needed when grinding a drill freehand. The drill is applied to the rim of the wheel with its cutting edge aligned with the axis of the spindle as shown at 'A'. The drill, now in contact with the wheel, is partially rotated as depicted at 'B', in order to impart the necessary 'backing off' or relief to the lip itself. After one lip has been ground satisfactorily the other is treated in the same way.

If the re-sharpened twist drill is to cut to size correctly it is important that the lips should remain a uniform length. The simple fixture illustrated at 'C' is sometimes used professionally to determine the uniformity of the lips. The diagram should be self-explanatory, but perhaps it should be explained that the upright member is painted with marking fluid and that the corner of each lip in turn is brought in contact with it so that lines can be scribed in the manner shown. When scribed lines are superimposed on each other the lip length can be considered uniform. No account,

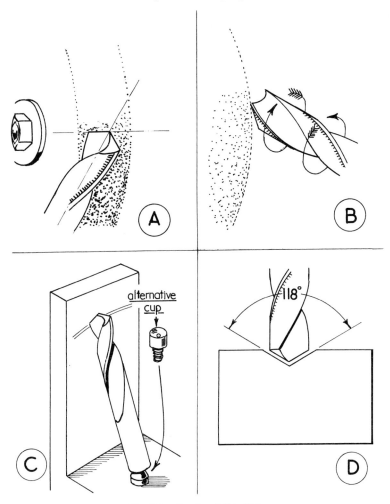

Fig. 5.3   Freehand Grinding.

however, is taken of the drill point angle. A simple check for this can be made by means of the simple gauge illustrated at 'D'. Referring to the uniformity of lip length the arrangement seen in the illustration *Fig. 5.4* can be used as a substitute for a more sophisticated fixture.

It is suggested that anyone who contemplates using freehand methods for drill grinding should first practice the movement that must be imparted to the drill by rolling it against a stationary

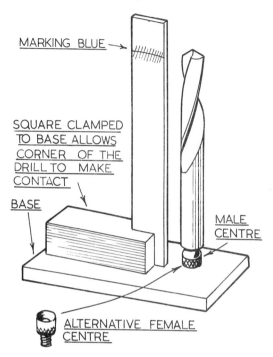

MARKING BLUE →

SQUARE CLAMPED
TO BASE ALLOWS
CORNER OF THE
DRILL TO MAKE
CONTACT

BASE

MALE
CENTRE

ALTERNATIVE FEMALE
CENTRE

Fig. 5.4   Device for checking lip length.

object such as an angle plate. In this way manual dexterity will gradually be acquired before attempting actual grinding on a wheel.

The Drill Grinding Jig

An experienced operative can always be relied upon to produce a tolerably satisfactory drill point by off-hand grinding. But there is no doubt that this practice cannot compare with the accuracy resulting from the employment of a properly designed drill grinding jig. Were it not so industry would hardly go to the lengths it does in setting up fully equipped well-staffed departments to ensure that any drills drawn from the tool stores are in first class condition.

Some years ago a design for a twist drill grinding jig by 'Duplex' was published in 'Model Engineer', and it is this device that is illustrated in *Fig. 5.5*, attached to a purpose made ball bearing grinding head driven by an independent electric motor.

The jigs used in industry are rather beyond the financial reach of

Fig. 5.5 'Duplex' Grinding Jig.

most users of the small workshop. However, there is at least one commercially made grinding jig specifically intended for amateur use. This is the device made by Messrs. G. Potts of Troutbeck in Windermere.

The fixture is depicted in the two illustrations *Fig. 5.6* and *5.7.* The latter giving an artists impression of the device with a drill in place. The jig is used to grind the drill point on the side of the wheel so needs to be secured to the base of the grinder in a way that will permit this procedure to be carried out.

In use, after the shank of the drill has been placed in the calliper gauge so that the jig can be correctly set, the drill itself is placed in the V-support with its cutting edge resting against the lip gauge. The drill is then fed forward by the screw seen behind the rear support while at the same time swinging the carrier so that the wheel gradually abrades the drill lip and imparts the necessary 'back-off'.

The drill needs to be examined from time-to-time to see when the grinding operation on the first lip has been completed. As soon as completion has been established the drill is replaced in the V-support or trough, the feed screw position being left where it was, and the second lip treated by gradually swinging the carrier towards

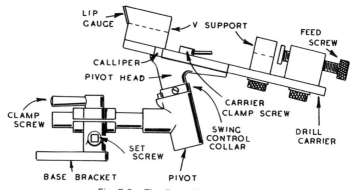

Fig. 5.6   The Potts Twist Drill Jig.

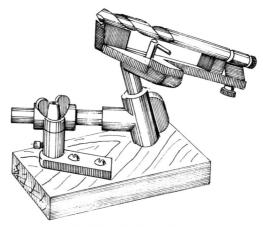

Fig. 5.7   The Potts Jig.

the wheel. In this way the grinding of the drill point will be uniform and the length of both lips the same.

Thinning the Drill Point

An examination of the drill point, when viewed end on, will show that there is an area at its centre which visually consists of a straight line joining both lips at an angle. This is called the 'chisel edge', a term perhaps conjuring up a condition of sharpness that does not exist. The larger the drill the worse the bluntness here, tending to a rubbing rather than a cutting action. In order to minimise the difficulty the procedure illustrated in *Fig. 5.8* is some-times adopted. This has the effect of reducing the obtuseness of the angle at the chisel edge so allowing the drill point to cut rather more freely.

Some years ago the author was engaged with others in investi-gating the standard drill point and its drawbacks when used in a particular application of interest to the aircraft industry. The particular problem was deep drilling in very high tensile steel with an accuracy requirement of 'no run out' if this was likely to be a practical possibility. The depth to be drilled was four inches, and a quarter of an inch diameter drill was used for the purpose.

A normal drill point was first employed, but this was a failure for two reasons. Firstly, the obtuseness of the chisel edge led to the point wearing out prematurely in such tough material. Secondly, the very shape of this chisel edge appeared to cause the drill to wander off course. Thinning the point in the customary manner tended to improve matters but the amount of run-out remained at an unacceptable level though the durability of the point itself had improved.

It was not, however, until the chisel edge had been modified in

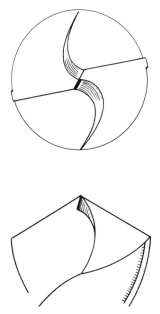

Fig. 5.8   Common method of thinning the drill point.

accordance with the diagrammatic representation depicted in *Fig. 5.9 at 'B'* that the run-out was reduced to the limits required. The maximum after several tests was a run-out of 0.003″ and in one case, there was no run-out at all.

The drill point before modification is illustrated at 'A' in *Fig. 5.9.* Modification is carried out with a knife-edge wheel applied to the drill point in the manner depicted in *Fig. 5.10.* If one is skilled enough, and has a steady hand, this grinding operation can be

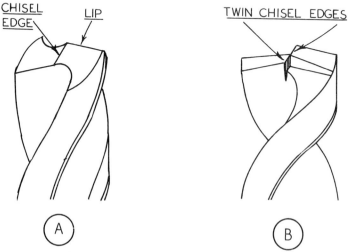

Fig. 5.9   Special method of point thinning.

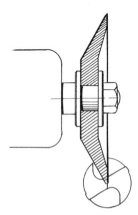

Fig. 5.10   Grinding the modified point.

performed freehand. But the advantages of the modification to the drill point, used in the lathe as well as the drilling machine, led the author to fit a special device to the machine he employs for cutter grinding. For general purposes only a few drill sizes need the modification since these can be used as pilot drills. In practice, if drills $\frac{1}{4}''$, $\frac{3}{8}''$ and $\frac{1}{2}''$ diameter are modified this will be sufficient. One should perhaps add that increased speed of penetration is an added bonus resulting from this modification.

Modifying the Drill Point for Brass

When straight-flute drills were available these could be used for drilling brass satisfactorily because their lips have no top rake, an essential condition under the circumstances. The twist drill on the other hand by its construction imparts a greater or lesser degree of top rake to its cutting edges. However, when setting out to drill

Fig. 5.11   Grinding the modified point.

brass components, this undesirable condition can be offset by the simple expedient illustrated in *Fig. 5.12*. All that is required is to stone the lips lightly in the area illustrated. This action will effectively reduce or even negative the rake angle and so allow the drill to cut without 'grabbing', a condition most often felt when opening out a hole that has previously been pilot-drilled.

Servicing Parallel Shank Drills

When standard jobbers drills are not firmly secured in a chuck their shanks may become scored and so unfit for accurate work. Fortunately for the most part, the shanks are soft so can readily be machined in order to correct any inaccuracy that may exist.

Servicing Taper Shank Drills

It sometimes happens that the shanks of drills having a Morse Taper become bruised for one reason or another. If accurate running of these drills is to be maintained the bruising cannot be allowed to persist. Usually a light treatment with a slip stone applied to the offending areas will cure the trouble. However, it may sometimes be necessary to lightly machine away the bruising provided this does not impair the general configuration of the taper.

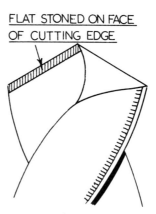

FLAT STONED ON FACE
OF CUTTING EDGE

Fig. 5.12   Modifying the lip when drilling brass.

CHAPTER SIX

USING THE DRILLING EQUIPMENT

Using the Drilling Equipment

Having considered those aspects of the matter that govern the design of the drilling machine, its installation and the servicing of its equipment, it is now time to consider the problems involved in the use of the drilling machine itself.

Holding the Work

Many of the drilling operations that have to be carried out are of a very simple nature and only need the part to be placed directly on the work table; if the work is large enough, being held in place by hand. It is important in this connection to remember that holding small parts in the hand when drilling can be most dangerous. If the drill jams in the work the possibility of sustaining severe cuts is a very real one.

To obviate this possibility the part should be held down by a simple clamp in the manner seen in the illustration *Fig. 6.1*. If it is possible to arrange the work so that the drill breaks through into any slots in the table, well and good; if this is not possible then a bolster of wood or metal must be placed under the work to protect the surface of the work table itself. But see to it that the bolster is flat and of a uniform thickness or the work will be thrown out of square with the axis of the drill.

The Machine Vice

It is not always possible or convenient however, to clamp work directly to the drill table. An accurate vice must then be employed. For small work the 'Eclipse' Vee-Vice depicted in *Fig. 6.2* is very suitable. It has also the added advantage that, when inverted, it becomes a long V-block whose use will be described later. A clamp

Fig. 6.1   A simple clamp for the work table.

Fig. 6.2   The 'Eclipse' Vee Vice.

to secure work placed in the V-block is provided together with a pair of round parallels designed to lift work off the surface of the vice itself. A pair of tenons running the length of the vice can be used to secure it to the work table as well as forming an anchorage for the clamp previously mentioned.

The small but accurate vice marketed by the Myford Engineering Company provides a first-class medium for securing small components on the drilling machine. The example illustrated in *Fig. 6.3* has been seen later. A typical application of the Myford vice is depicted in *Fig. 6.4*. Here the work is supported on a parallel packing piece to which it is clamped. The vice is substantial enough not to require clamping when small work is being drilled with drills say up to $\frac{1}{4}''$ diameter. Above this size it is well to secure the vice firmly.

V-Blocks

In the drilling machine one of the more useful devices is the V-block which enables the user to mount and secure shafts and

Fig. 6.3 The Myford Machine Vice.

Fig. 6.4   The Myford vice in use.

similar work for machining. V-blocks are available in many sizes
and many are used in matched pairs. The two blocks illustrated in
Fig. 6.5 are not matched accurately, though they may be used
together for purposes not needing the maximum accuracy. The
V-blocks seen in *Fig. 6.6* however, are matched and when used as a
pair will hold work truly parallel with the surface of the work table
on any machine where they may be employed. Moreover, they may
be turned on any of their faces and still maintain their individual
accuracy. A typical use for a V-block on the drilling machine is
illustrated in *Fig. 6.7*. The particular method of securing the block
to the work table will be noted.

The Setting Collar or Table Stop

One of the minor difficulties when using the drilling machine is
that of maintaining the table height in relation to the drill point,
while at the same time swinging the table to bring the work directly
under the drill. This vexation can be overcome if a table stop is
fitted to the column of the machine. With this in place, and locked
at the correct height, one can then swing the table around to bring
the work into position.

The simplest arrangement is that illustrated in *Fig. 6.8* where a
collar has been fitted below the table of an early Cowell drilling

Fig. 6.5   A pair of V-blocks.

Fig. 6.6   A pair of matched V-blocks.

machine. The Collar is similar to those seen in the illustration *Fig. 6.9*. A similar device was made by the author and fitted to a Pacera drilling machine. The column, here, is 3″ diameter so a collar of the type previously illustrated was really not a practical proposition because of the size of the material required. Instead, since a pair of

Fig. 6.7 A V-block in use on the drilling machine.

Fig. 6.8 Table Setting Collar fitted to the Cowell Drilling Machine.

Fig. 6.9   A group of split collars.

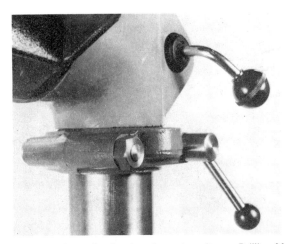

Fig. 6.10   The setting collar fitted to the authors Pacera Drilling Machine.

large bearing caps was available in a local garage, it was possible to produce the collar illustrated in *Fig. 6.10*. The component parts of the assembly may be seen in *Fig. 6.11* where the arrangement of the device should be clear. The two bearing caps were, of course

Fig. 6.11   Parts of the Pacera setting collar.

machined as a pair using the special bolts illustrated to hold them during the process.

It should, perhaps, be pointed out that a fixture of this type can be made to form the basis of a work table lift mechanism. Some of the floor based pillar drills such as the author's Pacera machine do not have this desirable feature.

Depth Stops and Depth Measuring Devices

One of the most important requirements in even the simplest of drilling machines is the ability to control the depth of the drill's penetration into the work as well as some ready method of measuring this depth if need be.

Regarding the first requirement, whenever the machined construction permits it an adjustable collar can be fitted to the upper end of the spindle and clamped so that when the collar touches the driving pulley the drill will have reached the required depth. The setting is, for the most part, carried out by means of a rule measurement taken in the manner illustrated in *Fig. 6.12* at 'A'. However, since the drilled depth required is generally in fractions of an inch, a setting gauge of the type illustrated in *Fig. 6.13* at 'B' may be used with advantage.

If marked off in fractions from $\frac{1}{8}''$ to $\frac{3}{16}''$ by increments of $\frac{1}{16}''$ up to half an inch, or perhaps $\frac{3}{4}$ of an inch, the gauge is usually small enough to hang on the machine, at some convenient point. Depths

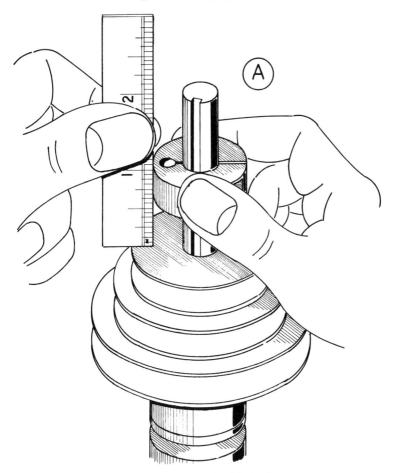

Fig. 6.12   Setting the drill depth.

above the gauge's maximum can be set by placing the device on a packing piece of known thickness. The setting of the stop is carried out with the point of the drill resting against the surface of the work.

Larger drilling machines of the American pattern such as the Pacera have a simple depth stop fitted to their quills consisting of a clamp supporting a pillar that passes through a lug cast on the head of the machine. The pillar is threaded and carries a pair of lock rings that can be adjusted to give the drilling depth required. The pillar usually carries rudimentary rule marking engraved on the

The Drilling Machine

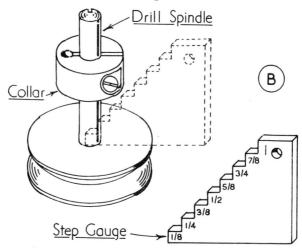

Drill Spindle

Collar

B

Step Gauge

7/8
3/4
5/8
1/2
3/8
1/4
1/8

Fig. 6.13   Setting the drill depth with a Step Gauge.

Fig. 6.14   Common depth stop and gauge for American Type Drilling Machine.

face of the pillar as may be seen in the diagram *Fig. 6.14* where the various parts of the device are depicted.

Quite apart from the fitting of depth stops it is advisable to provide some means of reading off directly the depth to which the drilling operation has progressed. In the original "Champion" machine, the feed shaft carried an adjustable engraved ring that could be used to read off the drilled depth. The two arrangements depicted in *Fig. 6.16* and *Fig. 6.17* respectively. The first is the device fitted by 'Duplex' to an early Cowell drilling machine whilst the second is the depth gauge applied to a 'Model Engineer' machine

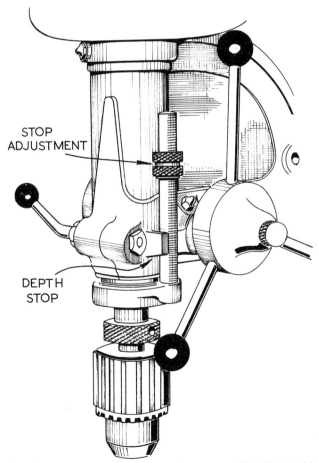

STOP
ADJUSTMENT

DEPTH
STOP

Fig. 6.15   Common depth stop and gauge for American Type Drilling Machine.

Fig. 6.17 Depth gauge fitted to the 'Model Engineer' Drilling Head.

Fig. 6.16 Depth gauge fitted to an early Cowell drilling machine.

head that was converted for use as a routing machine. The construction of both gauges will be evident from the two illustrations.

Modified Depth Gauge for American type machines

The depth gauge and stop already illustrated in *Fig. 6.14* whilst quite practical, is slow in operation when depth setting is concerned. A modification that allows the user to set the depth stop instantly is depicted in *Fig. 6.18*. The threaded pillar is replaced by a plain column keywayed axially. The depth stop slides on this column and is locked by the small ball handle seen in the illustration. The stop also carries a cursor that rides over a rule attached to the head of the machine so that the depth of drill penetration can be assessed. A key engaging the keyway in the column and fitted to the stop prevents

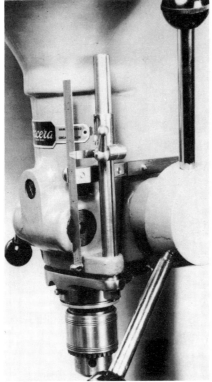

Fig. 6.18   Modified gauge and depth stop fitted to a Pacera drilling machine.

the latter from turning and so vitiating the reading of the rule. The assembly of the column and stop is illustrated in *Fig. 6.19*.

When using the rule to read off the drilled depth, it is obviously an advantage if one can adjust the position of the rule itself. By this means the rule can be set at a convenient location in relation to the cursor so enabling a reading to be taken more expeditiously.

The parts of the rule holder are depicted in *Fig. 6.20*. The fitting consists of an arm attached to the head of the drilling machine carrying a dovetailed clamp, in which a 6 inch rule can be secured after adjustment at any desired position.

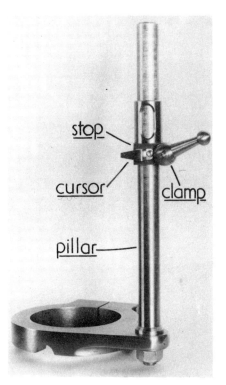

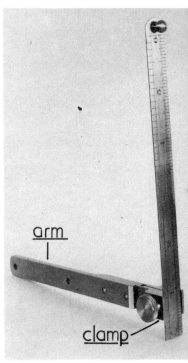

Fig. 6.20   The rule holder.

Fig. 6.19   Assembly of column and stop for
the modified depth stop.

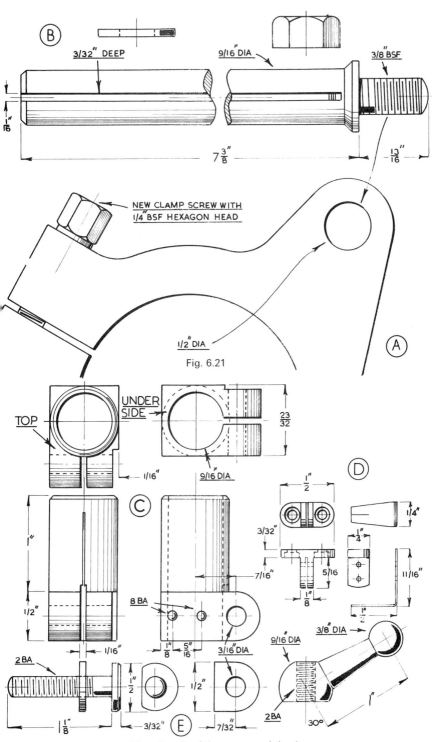

3/32" DEEP

9/16 DIA

3/8 BSF

7 3/8"

13/16"

NEW CLAMP SCREW WITH
1/4" BSF HEXAGON HEAD

1/2" DIA

Fig. 6.21

A

TOP

UNDER
SIDE

23/32

1/16"

9/16 DIA

C

D

1/2"

3/32"

7/16"

5/16

1/4"

1/4"

11/16"

8 BA

1/2"

1/16"

1/8"

5/16"

3/16" DIA

9/16 DIA

3/8 DIA

2 BA

1/2"

1/2"

2 BA

30°

1"

1 1/8"

3/32"

E

7/32"

Fig. 6.22   Details of the gauge and depth stop.

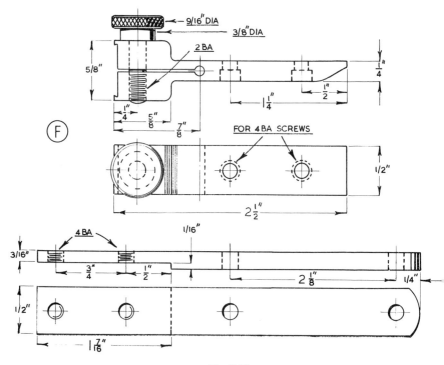

Fig. 6.23

CHAPTER SEVEN

FURTHER USE OF THE DRILLING MACHINE

Before we consider some of the more important operations that are carried out in the drilling machine the speeds at which drills should be run must be considered. The rating will depend on whether the drills are made from carbon steel or from high speed steel. Drill manufacturers usually provide speed tables based on the requirements of industry who require the maximum rate the drills will stand. For the most part, the drills used industrially are made from high-speed steel so the manufacturers base their tables on the use of this material. However, neither the amateur nor the user of the small workshop has need to drive his drills to their maximum capacity. Additionally, neither may feel inclined to invest solely in high-speed drills so the table that follows may be taken as a guide to permissible speeds:—

Drill dia. in inches	High Speed Steel Drills r.p.m.	Carbon Steel Drills r.p.m.
1/16	4000	1800
1/8	2000	900
3/16	1500	600
1/4	1100	450
5/16	900	340
3/8	750	280
7/16	650	240
1/2	550	210

These speeds may be doubled when drilling brass or aluminium, they are not, of course, absolute but will serve as a guide when arranging the drive to the drilling machine itself.

Cross Drilling

One of the more important processes that are carried out by a drilling operation is the forming of holes in a shaft and its mating component that can be used to secure one to the other usually by passing a pin through both. For the most part these holes pass through the centre of both components though there are times when they do not. The simplest way to ensure that both sets of holes are in alignment is to drill both parts together whenever this is possible. When 'drilling on assembly' as the phrase has it, is not a practical solution then, in default of a set of jigs, the work needs to be marked off and then set up correctly in the drilling machine.

A typical example is depicted in *Fig. 7.1* where the simplest method of arranging the work is illustrated. The work is first

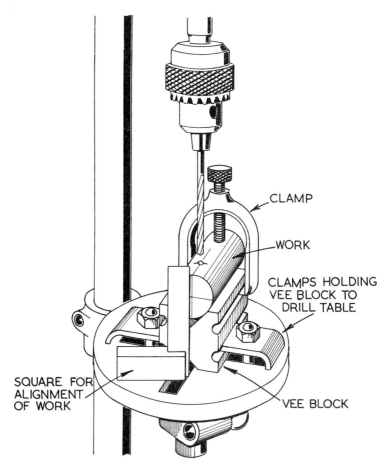

CLAMP

WORK

CLAMPS HOLDING
VEE BLOCK TO
DRILL TABLE

SQUARE FOR
ALIGNMENT
OF WORK

VEE BLOCK

Fig. 7.1   Setting work in a V-block.

marked off, as has been indicated previously, then set in a V-block so that it can be centre-drilled then drilled to size. As will be noted a square is used to check the location of the part with reference to the lines scribed upon it.

Before the work is set in place, however, it is essential to see that the V-block itself is central with the axis of the drill spindle. This may be assured very simply by adopting the method shown diagrammatically in *Fig. 7.2.*

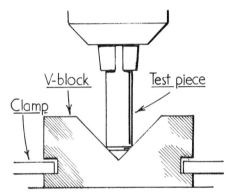

Fig. 7.2   Centring the V-block.

A test piece about half an inch diameter is set in the chuck and the spindle is lowered to bring the chamferred faces of the test pieces into contact with the V-block. The spindle is locked and the V-block clamps, that have previously been set loosely in place, are then tightened. Drilling can now take place.

Cross Drilling Jigs

Industrially, the cross-drilling of components is carried out in jigs specially made for the purpose, each one suited to the part concerned. There have been many attempts in the past to produce jigs that have a universal application, none of them particularly simple, so, before we go on to describe some of the less complicated devices that can be made by the amateur himself, it would be well to consider the simplest of all solutions to the problem. The method is one that is particularly applicable when cross-drilling is only an infrequent occurrence, and so the making of a universal jig may seem a waste of time.

While the procedure could no doubt be applied to larger components its principal use is in connection with small shafts. *Fig. 7.3* will demonstrate the method. All that is needed is a drill guide, the same diameter as the work, that can be gripped in the machine vice together with the work itself. The guide is drilled axially in the lathe to ensure concentricity and can readily be set in place either by mensuration or by viewing a marked-off line through the drilled hole if large enough, assuming this action will provide sufficient accuracy. An actual operation of this kind is illustrated in *Fig. 7.4*.

A development from this simple device is the fixture depicted in *Fig. 7.5*. It was designed to enable some small boring tools with inset cutters to be cross-drilled accurately. The fixture was designed to be mounted directly on the machine table when drilling at right angles to the axis of the boring bar, or in the machine vice when angular drilling is undertaken. Jigs of this type have to be tailor-made to the work in hand.

The first of the universal cross drilling jigs to be described is illustrated in *Fig. 7.6*. It was designed many years ago by Duplex who published a set of drawings that have recently been re-issued in 'The Amateurs Workshop' obtainable from Model and Allied Publications Ltd. of Hemel Hempstead. As will be observed the device is based on a V-block and is fitted with interchangeable guide bushes and a simple length stop. A development from this cross-drilling jig is seen in *Fig. 7.7*. It is based on a V-block marketed by the Myford Engineering Company. The same method of holding the work and the guide bush is retained but, because of the peculiar construction of the Myford V-block, a second clamp is provided to

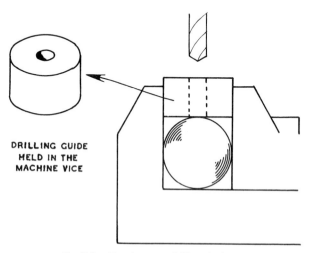

DRILLING GUIDE
HELD IN THE
MACHINE VICE

Fig. 7.3   Simple cross-drilling device.

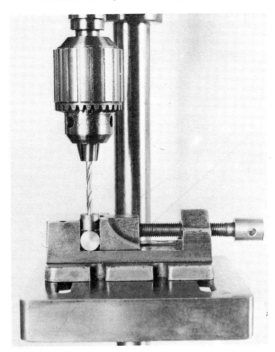

Fig. 7.4   Using the simple cross-drilling device.

Fig. 7.5   Cross-drilling jig for boring bars.

Fig. 7.6   The 'Duplex' Cross-drilling jig.

Fig. 7.7   Cross-drilling jig based on the Myford V-block.

hold the work in place. The length stop is much the same as that in the Duplex device, but it has been modified in the cause of simplification. A set of drawings for the complete jig appears later in the book.

Simple Jigs

Simple jigs often ease the production of components that would otherwise need to be marked off individually. Three such fixtures are seen in the illustration *Fig. 7.8*. On the left is a jig used for drilling some small pillars needed in model work. In the centre is a fixture to index the drill when some compressor valve guides were being machined. The jig on the right of the illustration was made to avoid having to mark off individually a number of safety valve bodies that had to be drilled.

An extension of the simple cross-drilling jig illustrated in *Fig. 7.8* is the little fixture depicted in *Fig. 7.9*. Its purpose will be clear from the illustration. As well as a length adjusting screw, which could with advantage have a lock screw of its own, there is a screw provided for locking the work during the drilling operation. Jigs of

Fig. 7.8   A group of simple jigs.

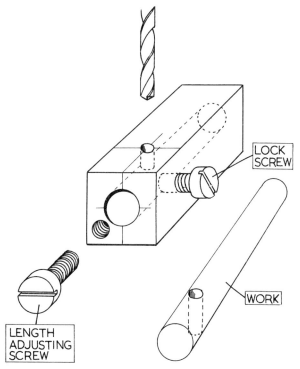

Fig. 7.9　Cross-drilling with adjustable stops.

Fig. 7.10　Jig for drilling cylinder flanges.

this pattern are readily made from square section material marked off and drilled appropriately, with holes tapped to take any requisite locking or length adjusting screws.

The two components illustrated in *Fig. 7.10* are the parts of a fixture made to enable the flanges of some small petrol engine cylinders to be drilled accurately. The jig plate on the left is registered with the base of the cylinder by means of the plug on the right. This plug fits the plate firmly and is made a push fit in the bore of the cylinder itself. In this way the jig plate is centralised and can be clamped in place for the drilling operation to be carried out. The plate itself is made the same size as the cylinder flange; this enables the plate to be correctly orientated. It is perhaps worth mentioning that the same jig was used to drill the cylinder seatings on the crankcase.

Quite apart from straightforward drilling the machine is used for other operations such as countersinking, counterboring and spotfacing. These three conditions of work are seen in the diagram *Fig. 7.11*.

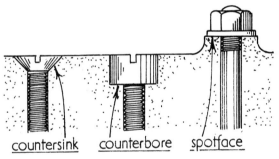

countersink   counterbore   spotface

Fig. 7.11   The Countersink, Counterbore and Spotface.

The Countersink

The countersink is an angular depression formed in the surface of the work to accept metal or woodscrews having heads machined to a corresponding angle. The angle is customarily made 90° though other angles are sometimes used. Commercially made countersinking cutters usually follow the pattern illustrated in *Fig. 7.12* to the left of the centre drill described in Chapter 4. It too, can be used for countersinking purposes but the included angle of the major part of the centre drill is 60° so it would need to be employed on some special duty.

If a commercial countersink of the type that has been illustrated

Fig. 7.12   A commercial countersink cutter.

is run at too high a speed, and the more so if the drilling machine in which the cutter is mounted is of light construction the surface of the countersink depression becomes roughened, to some extent repeating the pattern or formation of the countersink itself.

To illustrate what is meant a perfectly formed countersink in metal is depicted at 'A' in *Fig. 7.13*.

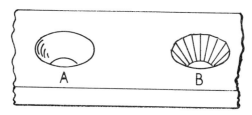

Fig. 7.13   Correctly formed and malformed countersinks.

At 'B' however, the cutter has been run too fast, 'chatter' has taken place and the resulting countersink has become malformed. As to the speed at which the operation is most satisfactorily carried out, this clearly depends on the diameter of the countersink itself. In general the slower the spindle turns the better, 60 to 100 r.p.m. are speeds that can be used with success. The work of course needs to be lubricated with lard oil or a straight mineral cutting oil.

There is a form of countersinking tool, however, that is proof against 'chatter'. This tool is based on the D-bit, well known to turners for its ability to drill a perfectly straight hole. It is illustrated in *Fig. 7.14*, together with a sample of work carried out by it and the metal shavings it produces. The tool cuts freely, produces a fine finish and is best run slowly, the proportions of a typical example are given in *Fig. 7.15*. This type of countersink is used industrially,

Fig. 7.14   A non-chattering countersink.

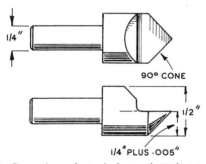

Fig. 7.15   Proportions of a typical non-chattering countersink.

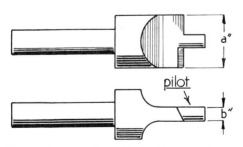

Fig. 7.16   Proportions of a simple counterbore.

and is made as a commercial product, but for some reason or other does not seem to be available from tool merchants.

The Counterbore

When it becomes necessary to produce a seating for cheese-head screws that leaves the top of them level with the surface of the work, one needs to use a counterbore. In its simplest form, which is a suitable type to copy when making the tools for oneself, the counterbore appears as depicted in *Fig. 7.16*. The dimension 'a' is the diameter of the screw head to be seated, while 'b' is a measurement that will allow the pilot to pass into the clearance hole for the screw itself. The pilot must run free without shake so if the pilot is made the same diameter as the drill used to form the hole then it will run with the right clearance.

A set of counterbores to suit standard screws are readily made from silver steel rod; these can be produced one at a time as requisite and hardened and tempered to a light straw colour. It sometimes happens however that non-standard screws have to be accommodated. These either have non-standard heads or standard heads with perhaps an oversize threaded portion. Cutters with detachable pilots are then indicated. A pair of them are illustrated in *Fig. 7.17* whilst the manner of making such cutters is depicted in *Fig. 7.18*.

Spot-face Cutters

Spot-facing is a practice adopted to provide a proper seating for any nuts and washers used to secure parts together. The seatings are, for the most part, lugs cast on the parts in the manner shown by *Fig. 7.11*. Cutters for the purpose are much the same as those used for counterboring but, have cutting faces larger in diameter than those of a counterbore. They usually have three or four cutting edges.

Tapping in the Drilling Machine

Threaded holes tapped in pieces of mechanism need to be quite square axially. If the tapping operation is carried out freehand there can be no guarantee that true axial alignment has been preserved. But when the drilling machine is pressed into service the tap, being mounted in the drill chuck, is kept perfectly upright so produces an accurately threaded hole.

The simplest method of converting the drilling machine for the purpose of tapping is to fit its spindle with a handle so that it can

Fig. 7.17   A pair of counterbores with detachable pilots.

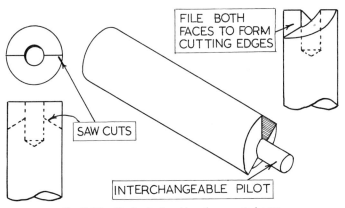

FILE BOTH FACES TO FORM CUTTING EDGES

SAW CUTS

INTERCHANGEABLE PILOT

Fig. 7.18   Method of making the counterbores.

be turned by hand. A suitable handle is illustrated in *Fig. 7.19*. This is designed to fit over the spindle of such machines as the 'Champion' and the 'Cowell'. The hexagon head screw seen projecting from the body of the device has its point turned down so that it will engage the spindle keyway without damaging the spindle itself.

The leverage of the handle can be adjusted by slackening the

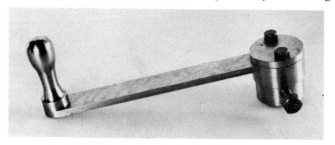

Fig. 7.19   Tapping handle for the drilling machine.

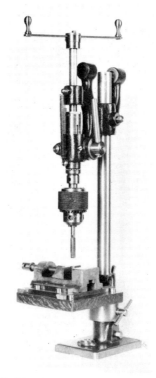

Fig. 7.20   Modified handle fitted to a converted drilling machine.

clamp screws at the top of the body, sliding the arm along under the cap and re-securing it at the desired point. A later design of the handle provided a pair of finger grips since these were found to be beneficial. It is this version of the handle that is illustrated in *Fig. 7.20* attached to the spindle of a drilling machine that has been converted for tapping purposes. Detail drawings of the simple handle are given in *Fig. 7.21* and *7.22*.

Tapping Operations

One of the commonest operations that can, with advantage, be carried out in the drilling machine is the tapping of nuts which may have had to be specially made for some purpose or other. The blanks for such nuts are first produced by a drilling and turning operation carried out in the lathe. The blanks are then transferred to the drilling machine for the tapping operation. In order to carry out this work easily they are dropped one at a time into the fixture seen in the illustration *Fig. 7.23*. This device was designed to

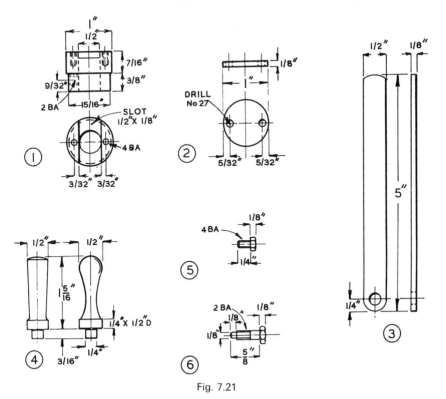

Fig. 7.21

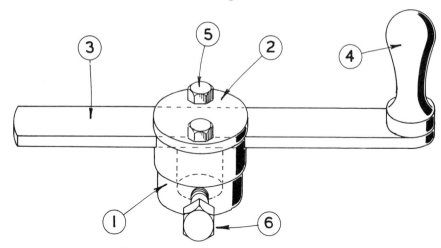

Fig. 7.22   Details of the simple tapping handle.

Fig. 7.23   Fixture for tapping nuts in the drilling machine.

accommodate standard hexagon material and has been provided with means of adjustment allowing the nut blanks to be inserted freely. As will be noticed a nut tap is set in the chuck. This is a form of tap that has a shank slightly smaller than the drilled bore of the nut blanks. Consequently, if the tap is allowed to pass clear through them a quantity of finished nuts will collect on the shank from which from time to time they can be removed.

The average drilling machine available to the amateur has only a narrow 'throat'. The throat is the distance from the centre of the drill spindle to the column so where this measurement is restricted the drilling of large area components is a difficult if not impossible proposition. One solution is illustrated in *Fig. 7.24* this involves the use of parts of two simple drilling machines which, when assembled together, form a composite whole with a greatly increased capacity for drilling work such as large plates. The drilling machines involved in the modification depicted are 'The Model Engineer' and the 'Tom Senior' tools. As will be seen a surface plate serves as the work table.

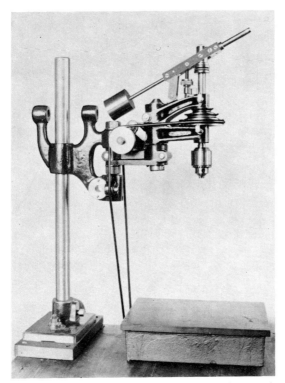

Fig. 7.24   Improvised arrangement for drilling large surfaces.

CHAPTER EIGHT

LOW-VOLTAGE ELECTRIC DRILLS

The practicability of machines powered by low-voltage electrical supplies is a subject that has exercised the author for many years. Having been involved many years ago in the production of sets for the generating of low-voltage electricity, and later in the solution of troubles that afflicted low-voltage aircraft electrical equipment, the possibilities of using some of it in the workshop became apparent to him.

There seem always to be examples of this material available on the surplus market where it may be bought for a fraction of its original cost. The excellence of the items on offer cannot be questioned both as to design and manufacture, so, if suitable equipment is chosen, quite practical machines can be devised.

It would be quite impossible, in a single chapter, to give detailed instruction for the making of any particular tool. All that will be attempted, therefore, is to arouse interest in the subject by describing a couple of tools that have been made by the author.

Low-voltage Electrical Supplies

In order to operate low-voltage machines a suitable electrical supply must be available in the workshop. The simplest method of providing this is to install a transformer of adequate capacity with, additionally, a rectifier located alongside to give the user a direct current supply when needed. The transformer should have a possible output of some 750 k.v.a. at 12–28 volts a.c. while the rectifier should be capable of supplying 12–16 amperes at up to 24 volts d.c. In the author's workshop the transformer/rectifier system is made portable so that the electrical leads from its low-voltage side can be kept as short as possible.

In this connection it should be noted that considerable power from a low-voltage source involves a heavy current consumption, and that any external cable resistance would materially diminish the current passing. The author's equipment is illustrated in *Fig. 8.1.*

Fig. 8.1   The Transformer and Rectifier.

The transformer itself is mounted in a wooden box to the side of which the rectifier is attached. In the illustration both the alternating and direct current sides of the unit are seen in use, with the d.c. output controlled through a variable resistance normally used in connection with automatic feeds to certain machine tools in the workshop. The transformer is one of a type that has its primary and secondary windings completely isolated from one another. Under these circumstances no leakage of mains voltage to the secondary winding is possible unless a complete breakdown of insulation between the windings has taken place, a somewhat unlikely happening. On the other hand, while perfectly capable of providing the necessary electrical energy, the auto-transformer as it is called has no separate windings but consists of a continuous series of turns forming one single winding having tappings at predetermined intervals. The mains then are therefore, in direct contact with any apparatus connected to its output terminals. The two types of transformer are depicted diagrammatically in *Fig. 8.2.*

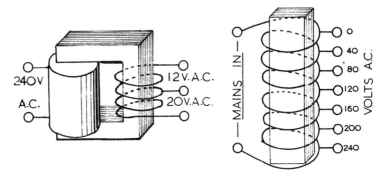

Fig. 8.2   Schematic Transformer diagram.

Both types are in use by the author and have voltage outputs of the order indicated in the illustration. The auto-transformer, however, has to be used with discretion.

The Series Wound Motor

The class of motor that is suitable for adaption is one that will give a short time rating of one-third h.p. is of sturdy construction and is series wound. The motor, therefore, will resemble those used for starting the engine of an automobile. The series wound motor, illustrated diagrammatically in *Fig. 8.3*, has the advantage that it

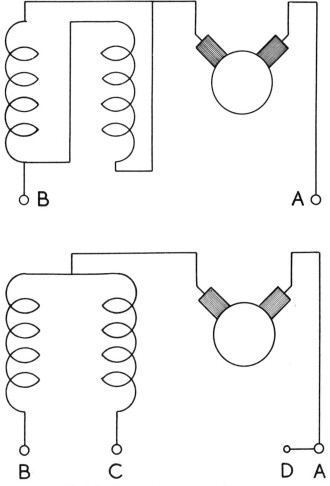

Fig. 8.3   Diagram of series wound motors.

will run on either alternating or direct current, the latter being the more useful if protracted running is to be expected. The construction is such that alternating current has a rather greater heating effect than has direct current.

Low-voltage Electrical Hand Drill

The machine depicted in *Fig. 8.4* was evolved from a motor designed for use with the Bofors gun. In addition to certain

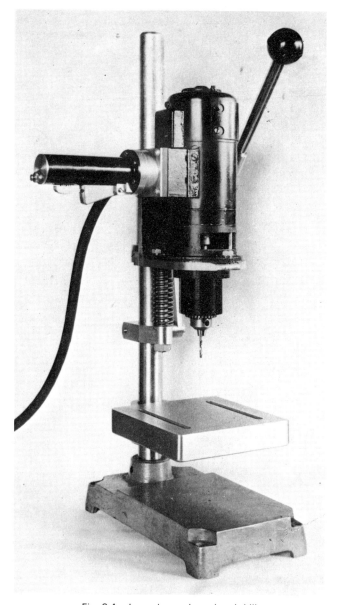

Fig. 8.4   Large low voltage hand drill.

mechanical modifications a switch capable of handling comparatively heavy currents had to be evolved. The resulting device is
depicted in *Fig. 8.5* and illustrated as a general arrangement in
Fig. 8.6. The contact system is self-cleaning, following the lines of the

Fig. 8.5   Heavy current switch.

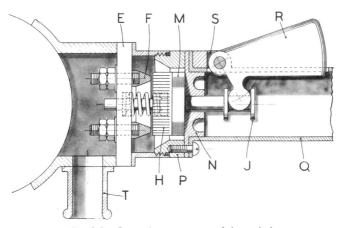

Fig. 8.6   General arrangement of the switch.

starter switches once used in motor cars. These comprised a pair of cups, slotted to allow a hinging action whenever they are brought into contact with two metal segments placed in series with the motor and the source of electrical energy. Experience has shown that this form of switch has a very long life and requires no maintenance.

The details of the switch fitted to the author's low-voltage drill were published in 'Model Engineer' many years ago and it is the illustration of the switch that then appeared which is reproduced here, in *Fig. 8.7*. The switch forms part of the handle 'Q' into which its components are built. The plunger 'J' carries the two concentric cups 'H' and is spring-loaded. It is operated by the lever 'R' which pushes the cups into contact with the metal segments 'F'. This action closes the electrical circuit and starts the motor. There is a

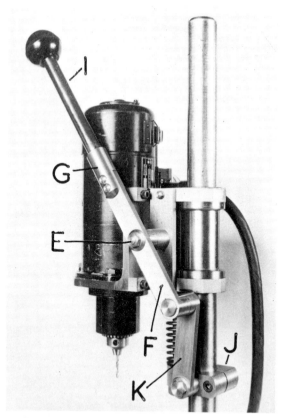

Fig. 8.7   The author's large low-voltage hand drill.

very large area of metal in contact here, so the chance of electrical arcing is virtually nullified.

Mounting the Drill Chuck

One of the advantages of the particular motor chosen was the facility with which a drill chuck could be mounted. Only two small components are needed to secure the chuck and these are seen in the illustration *Fig. 8.8*. The motor itself is provided with a short shaft 'A' in which a key is set. The sleeve 'B' is made a sliding fit over the shaft and is held in place by the barrel nut 'C'. The sleeve is, of course, tapered to fit the bore of the chuck itself.

The completed machine was used as a hand drill for some time before it was decided to provide it with a stand so that it could be employed as a drilling machine when needed. Apart from devising the stand itself, the basis of which is the base, column and table of an old Cowell drilling machine, it was necessary to fit the existing starting switch with a rapid action lock-and-release device that would enable the user once the motor had been started to employ his hands for holding the work and feeding the drill. This fitting is

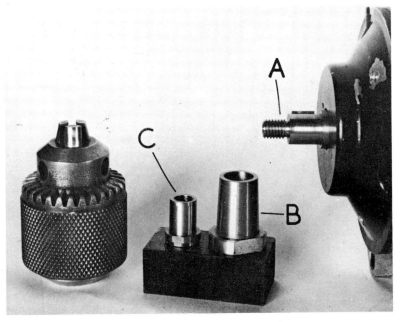

Fig. 8.8   Mounting for the drill chuck.

illustrated in *Fig. 8.9* and depicted sectioned in *Fig. 8.10* an illustration from the original publication. The Body 'N' fits the tubular
handle containing the switch previously described. It houses the
spring-loaded detent 'Q' which bears on an extension to the original
switch lever. With the device in operation the detent engages a
notch in the lever when this is fully depressed. If the machine again
is to be used as a hand drill the detent can be held out of engagement
by the finger nut 'R'. When the detent is in action it can be released
by the thumb piece 'S'.

Fig. 8.9   The switch detent.

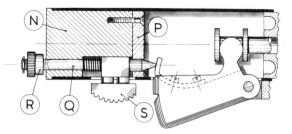

Fig. 8.10   Section of the switch.

A Small Electric Hand Drill

The basis of the device illustrated in *Fig. 8.11* is an electric motor
made by Bosch of Stuttgart, and forming a part of the electrical

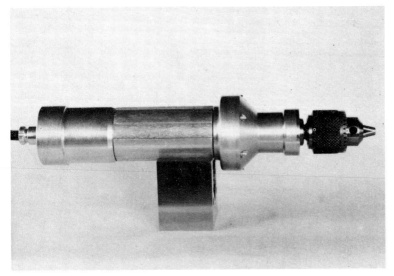

Fig. 8.11   Small low-voltage hand drill.

equipment built in to a German aircraft brought down near the author's house during the last war. As might be expected it is a beautifully made machine having a shape well suited to being held in the hand; fortunately it was virtually undamaged in the crash. In service the motor appeared to have been submerged in the engine cooling system; it was necessary, therefore, to carry out some modifications to get rid of unwanted structural features and to fit the body of the machine so that it would accept a specially designed epicyclic reduction gearbox at the driving end. While at the opposite end of the motor a dust cover had to be fitted over the brush gear. This cover also houses a cable grip. The modification to the driving end of the casing and the dust cover are illustrated in *Fig. 8.12* and *Fig. 8.13* respectively.

The Epicyclic Gearbox

This gearbox is a self-contained unit attached directly to the driving end of the motor. It is comprised as depicted in *Fig. 8.14* of two halves of the casing 'A' and 'B' housing the bearing assembly for the shaft 'E'. A tubular distance piece separates the bearings themselves which are held in place by the cap 'B1'. The nut 'F' secures the inner races of the bearings, sandwiching them between a shoulder machined on the shaft and the nut itself while the distance piece ensures that the races are not over-compressed.

A spider member 'C' is machined on the end of the drive shaft to carry the three planetary pinions 'D2' that mesh with the driving gear 'D1' mounted on the end of the motor shaft.

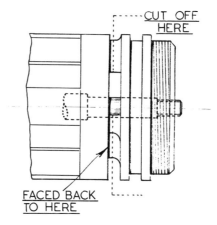

Fig. 8.12   Modification to the motor casing (driving end).

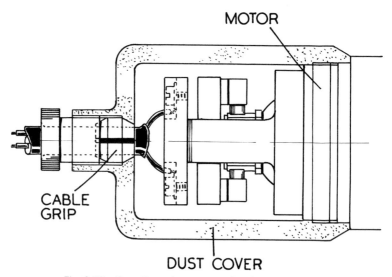

Fig. 8.13   Dust Cover for motor casing (commutator end).

The Chuck Mounting

The illustration *Fig. 8.14* also demonstrates the method of mounting the drill chuck. A split tapered collet is made a sliding fit on the drive shaft abutting against a shoulder machined upon it. The chuck itself is secured by a screw passing into the axis of the drive shaft.

To return to the gearbox itself. The parts of the device are illustrated in *Figs. 8.15–8.18*. The ring gear seen in *Fig. 8.15* was

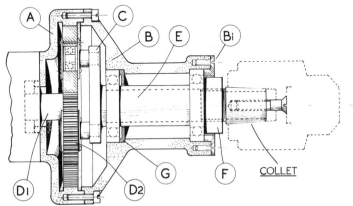

Fig. 8.14   Section of epicyclic gear-box.

Fig. 8.15   Parts of the epicyclic gear-box.

machined from the gearbox material, a hard light alloy, using a shaping operation carried out with a form tool mounted in the lathe toolpost. This class of operation is described in 'The Shaping Machine' published by Model and Allied Publications Limited.

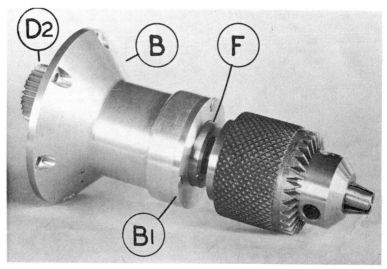

Fig. 8.16   Parts of the epicyclic gear-box.

Fig. 8.17   Parts of the epicyclic gear-box.

The Planetary Gears

The arrangement of the planetary gear system is, perhaps, of some interest. The gears were machined from Nylon rod and, as may be seen in *Fig. 8.19*, are each supported on a single ball race held in place by steel shrouds held together by rivets passed through the gears themselves.

It is hoped that by describing a simple machine with its drill chuck running at motor speed, and then detailing a smaller hand drill fitted with a reduction gearbox, enough interest will have been generated to encourage some readers to investigate these matters for themselves.

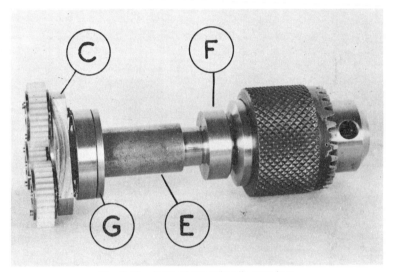

Fig. 8.18   Parts of the epicyclic gear-box.

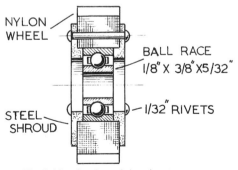

Fig. 8.19   Section of the planet gears.

CHAPTER NINE

LATHE DRILLING ATTACHMENTS

The lathe itself is a drilling machine in its own right, and has been used as such, probably for centuries, with work mounted against the tailstock or later on the saddle.

It is, however, sometimes convenient to have the work secured to the headstock and to operate on it with attachments secured to the saddle or forming an addition to the tailstock.

Saddle Mounted Attachments

The 'Model Engineer' drilling machine can be used to provide a saddle mounted attachment by simply removing the head from its column and supporting it on a mounting secured to the cross slide. An example of such an arrangement is illustrated in *Fig. 9.1*. Here

Fig. 9.1   Drill head mounted on Drummond Lathe.

Fig. 9.2   Mounting for the drill head.

the drill head is seen attached to the saddle of a $3\frac{1}{2}''$ Drummond lathe and driven from an overhead shaft set behind and above it. The mounting itself is depicted in *Fig. 9.2.* It comprises a column 'A' attached to the Base Plate 'B' by means of which the device is attached to the saddle. A clamp 'C' is free to move up and down the column and so may be used to adjust the drilling head to lathe centre height after it has been secured to the spigot 'D'. In this way the centring arrangements follow accepted Drummond practice for setting the tool at lathe centre height.

This device has been much used for light end-milling and spot-drilling rings of holes at some definite pitch circle diameter, with spacing controlled by simple dividing equipment attached to the mandrel while the pitch circle setting is measured by the cross slide micrometer index.

These are matters that are dealt with comprehensively in 'The Amateur's Workshop' published by Model and Allied Press Limited. For simple dividing one can make use of a suitable lathe change wheel mounted on the end of the mandrel, engaging with it a detent at appropriate intervals. For example, supposing six spaces were needed and a 60T gear had been set at the tail of the mandrel then the detent would need to be engaged with every tenth tooth space.

A more versatile arrangement is seen in the illustration *Fig. 9.3,* where the dividing head attached to the author's Myford lathe is

Fig. 9.3   Dividing head on Myford Lathe.

depicted. This device can be made to engage a wide range of change wheels. The pitch of the worm attached to the operating shaft is such that one turn of the handle advances the change wheel one tooth, so by making the necessary number of turns each division can be quickly made.

Electrically Driven Spot Drilling Attachment

The equipment illustrated in *Fig. 9.4* is a development from a small drilling spindle mounted on the cross slide and driven from an overhead shaft, see *Fig. 9.5*. By introducing a small reduction gearbox, and providing a motor mounting upon it, it has been possible to run this drilling spindle from the low-voltage supply in the author's workshop. It is usually fitted with a slocomb centre drill so that it can be used to spot drill groups of holes in components gripped in the chuck.

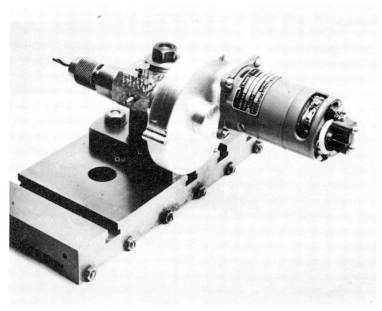

Fig. 9.4　Electrically driven spot drilling attachment.

Fig. 9.5　The original back toolpost drilling head.

The attachment is mounted on the column of the lathe back toolpost whence it can quickly be removed or replaced when needed.

Tailstock Drilling Attachments

Workshops engaged on development or light instrument work have in the past, been interested in attachments that convert the 'tailstock' of the lathe into a self-contained drilling machine. A basic requirement for satisfactory working is that the tailstock spindle should be lever-operated, for it is advisable that the small drills, for which the equipment is suitable, should be quickly cleared of swarf during the drilling operation. In addition the sensitivity that lever feed provides is a great asset when drilling.

The attachment to be described was originally fitted to an early Winfield lathe and it is the modified tailstock of this tool that is illustrated in *Fig. 9.6.* As will be seen the hand wheel was retained

Fig. 9.6   Tailstock modified for lever feed.

for use when required, and the lever anchorage could be rotated around the axis of the tailstock to bring the operating lever into a convenient position for working. The complete drilling equipment mounted on the modified tailstock could be set on the column of an old drilling machine and is thus illustrated in *Fig. 9.7*.

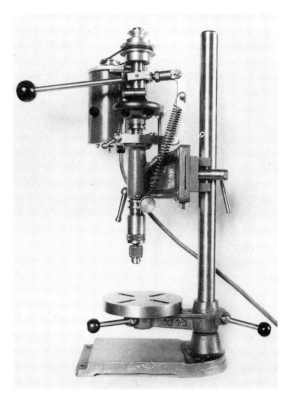

Fig. 9.7   Tailstock drilling attachment mounted on vertical column.

The device was subsequently transferred to the tailstock of a Myford lathe where it is seen depicted in *Fig. 9.8*. This lathe is fitted with a Cowell lever-feed system and has a long spindle that imparts added rigidity to the equipment. The motor is mounted behind the tailstock on a bracket clamped to the spindle, the construction of the bracket, which is illustrated in *Fig. 9.9* and *Fig. 9.10,* being of a nature that allows the tension of the endless elastic belt to be adjusted at will.

A typical operation for which the device is useful is that seen in

Fig. 9.8   Tailstock drilling attachment on Myford Lathe.

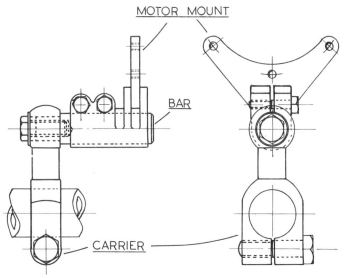

Fig. 9.9   Motor mounting bracket.

Fig. 9.10 Motor mounting bracket.

Fig. 9.11. Here a number of small taper pins, mounted in an adapter caught in a collet chuck, are being drilled axially for some one-and-a-half inches in length to accept a 1 m/m (0.040″) cable. The contra-rotating principle for drilling is employed, the drill spindle rotating at 5000 r.p.m. in one direction while the lathe mandrel turns in the opposite hand at some 500 r.p.m. By this method it is usually possible to produce axially true drilled holes.

Lubrication of the drill and the work is provided for by the nozzle seen pointing down in the illustration. This forms part of a mist lubrication device designed originally to assist in the sculpturing of large aircraft components.

A sectional view of the attachment is depicted in *Fig. 9.12*. The device consists of two distinct assemblies, the driver and the driven component, mounted at opposite ends of the tailstock mandrel and

Fig. 9.11   The drilling attachment in use.

connected together by a spindle 'H' running in bearings at each end of the equipment. At the forward end the housing 'A' is the location for a pair of ball races held in place by the ring nut 'D' which also serves as a dust cap. Distance pieces are provided to ensure accurate end location of the races. The housing is mounted on a hollow Morse taper sleeve to which it is secured by the clamp 'F' and clamp screw 'G'.

At the driving end the light alloy pulley 'K' also forms the housing for a pair of ball races, these are provided with the customary separators and the whole is held together by the screwed dust cover 'N'.

The hollow spigot 'I' fits into the rear end of the tailstock mandrel where it is secured by a small allen grub screw. The spigot has a pair of bronze bushes let into each end, these centralise the spindle 'H' which has a slot machined across its end in congruence with a similar slot machined in the pulley. The dog 'O', machined to conform with the two slots and held in place by a screw set axially in the spindle, can thus transmit the drive from one assembly to the other.

A further development of the idea is illustrated in *Fig. 9.13*. This shows the equipment as fitted to a **Pultra** instrument lathe. In this

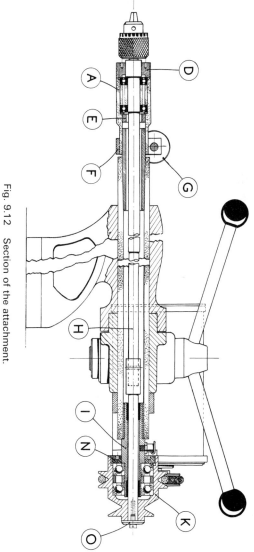

Fig. 9.12 Section of the attachment.

Fig. 9.13   Attachment fitted to the Pultra Lathe.

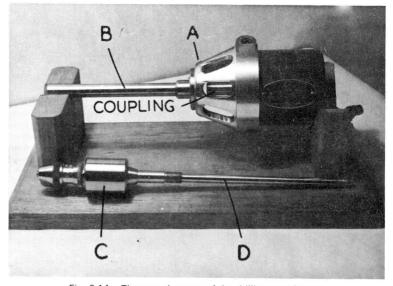

Fig. 9.14   The two elements of the drilling attachment.

instance the driving motor is set directly in line with the drill spindle and is coupled to it by a simple dog clutch consisting of a sleeve and cross-pin. The two elements forming the complete set-up is depicted in *Fig. 9.14*. The tailstock of the Pultra lathe is bored to accept collet chucks; the Adapter 'C' is therefore machined to conform with this design feature. The spindle 'D' is fitted with the smallest size in Albrecht chucks since the equipment as a whole was needed for the drilling of small stainless steel components. The Tube 'B' is threaded internally to engage the Adaptor 'C', so by turning the motor and its housing 'A' the assemblies can be locked in place.

The attachment is shown sectioned in *Fig. 9.15*. The general design of the attachment follows closely that of the device fitted to the Myford lathe and already described.

The driving motor is an ex-aircraft machine running at 24 volts d.c. and made by Delco. It has a maximum speed capacity of some 5000 r.p.m. and is controlled by a rheostat mounted in the box seen in the illustration. It is perhaps worth recording that the tapered end of the spindle on which the drill chuck is mounted was machined in situ, the driving motor providing the power. The operation involved inverting the turning tool and, of course, setting over the top slide to the angle required.

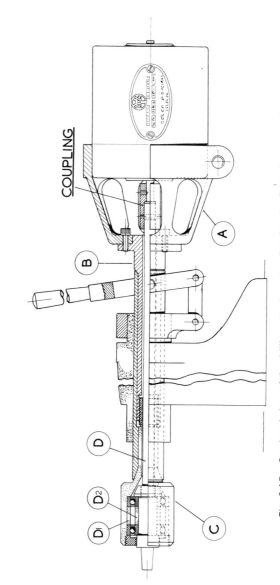

COUPLING

Fig. 9.15　Sectional view of the drilling attachment as fitted to the Pultra instrument lathe.

CHAPTER TEN

ADDITIONS TO THE DRILLING MACHINE

In earlier chapters we have already described some additions, many of them of a simple nature, that will contribute to the satisfactory working of the drilling machine. The list of refinements was not then exhausted so it is now proposed to fill in any gaps that still exist, and to amplify, perhaps, or add to any information already given.

Depth Stops

The importance of adequate depth stops has already been stressed earlier in the book. Without this provision it is extremely difficult if not impossible, to drill, for example, a series of holes all of a similar depth. When the spindle projects through and slides in the driving pulley as is the case of the Champion and the Cowell drilling machines, a simple split collar can be set on the spindle and locked at whatever point provides the correct drill depth. A stop of this nature is not a practical fitment for those drilling machines that have the lever feed arrangements depicted in the illustration *Fig. 10.1*. Instead, the device illustrated in *Fig. 10.2*, and fitted to the 'Model Engineer' drilling machine, will serve as an example of a possible solution to the difficulty. The basis of this device is a bracket 'D' that clamps to the head of the machine being secured by the clamp screw 'E'. The stop itself consists of three parts, the stud 'A' the adjustable stop 'B' and a pair of rollers 'C' that make contact with the stop which is spring loaded to ensure that it retains position when set.

The stop 'B' is friction loaded by means of a spring-and-plunger device located under the grub screw seen at the edge of the stop. The bracket carrying the stop mechanism can also be used to mount a rule by means of which the drilling depth can be measured. A clamp contracted by the thumb screw 'G' grips the rule 'F' which

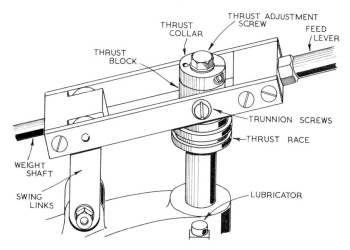

Fig. 10.1   Drilling Machine overhead lever feed.

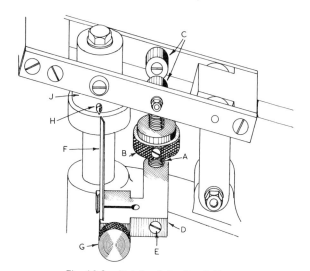

Fig. 10.2   Details of the Depth Stop.

can thus be adjusted in relation to the pointer 'H' set in the feed thrust block 'J'. Details are given in *Fig. 10.3*.

For the class of drilling machine in which the spindle does project through the driving pulley the split clamp stop depicted in *Fig. 10.4 at 'A'* has already been described. A simpler device, that

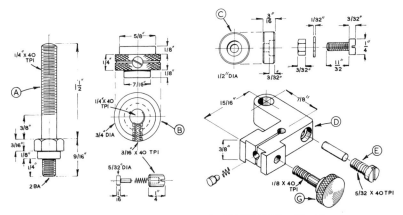

Fig. 10.3   Depth stop fitted to the "M.E." Drilling Machine.

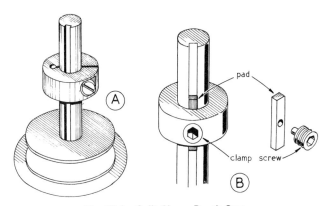

Fig. 10.4   Split Clamp Depth Stop.

may commend itself to those who wish to employ something perhaps a little more easily made, is the stop illustrated at 'B'. The stop is a solid component fitted with a clamp screw engaging a pad that slides in the drill spindle keyway. As soon as the clamp screw is tightened the pad is forced into the keyway locking the whole assembly solid.

Measuring the drilled depth

Some drilling machines available in the past have the bottom lug of their head casting split so that a screw passing through the

sawcut and engaging the back of the lug, can be used to adjust the
bearing of the quill in the lug itself.

This arrangement provides a convenient way of mounting a rule
alongside the quill so that the movement of the drill spindle can be
read off directly. A typical set-up is illustrated in *Fig. 10.5*.

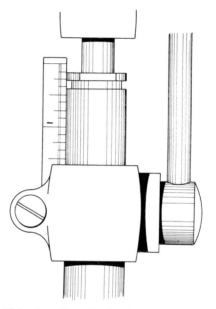

Fig. 10.5   Rule Mounting for the Drilling Machine.

Varying the drill speed

The simple type of drilling machine is somewhat restricted as to
the amount of speed variation it can provide. However, a simple
modification can do much to alleviate this lack. The illustrations
Fig. 10.6 and *Fig. 10.7* show a method that has been applied to the
Cowell and Champion drilling machines. The view of the modification showing the system in plan is the arrangement also used in
connection with the Champion machine, while the alternative view
demonstrates a later version of the Cowell modification.

The Cowell Drilling Machine Speed Range

As will be observed from a consideration of the diagram and
speed table *Fig. 10.8*, ten speeds are available varying from 145

Fig. 10.6   Cowell Speed Range.

r.p.m. to 4300 r.p.m., a flexibility that should satisfy most amateur
and small workshop needs. In order to obtain this variation a 2-
step driving pulley is fitted to the motor shaft, the drive to the
countershaft pulley 'B' being by $\frac{1}{4}''$ round leather belting, thereafter
two $\frac{3}{8}''$ V-ropes are employed to transmit the drive to the drill
spindle itself.

Details of the parts needed for the older Cowell machines are
given in the illustrations *Fig. 10.9*, *Fig. 10.10* and *Fig. 10.11*. The
cast-iron bracket 'A' depicted in *Fig. 10.9* is in fact a spare work
table bracket and was obtained from Messrs. E. W. Cowell of
Watford. It needs to be drilled and spotfaced to enable the flat mild
steel support 'B' for the intermediate pulley to be secured to it. A
small bracket 'C', illustrated in *Fig. 10.10*, is attached to the support
and is free to move along it. In this way the position of the intermediate pulley mounted on the pillar 'D' can be adjusted to provide

Fig. 10.7   Champion Speed Range.

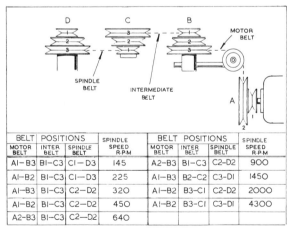

| BELT | POSITIONS | | SPINDLE | BELT | POSITIONS | | SPINDLE |
MOTOR BELT	INTER BELT	SPINDLE BELT	SPEED R.P.M	MOTOR BELT	INTER BELT	SPINDLE BELT	SPEED R.P.M
AI–B3	BI–C3	CI–D3	145	A2–B3	BI–C3	C2–D2	900
AI–B2	BI–C3	CI–D3	225	AI–B3	B2–C2	C3–DI	1450
AI–B3	BI–C3	C2–D2	320	AI–B2	B3–C1	C2–D2	2000
AI–B2	BI–C3	C2–D2	450	AI–B2	B3–CI	C3–DI	4300
A2–B3	BI–C3	C2–D2	640				

Fig. 10.8   Speed Table for Cowell Drilling Machine.

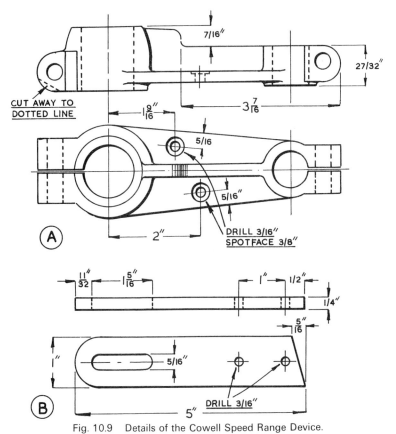

Fig. 10.9   Details of the Cowell Speed Range Device.

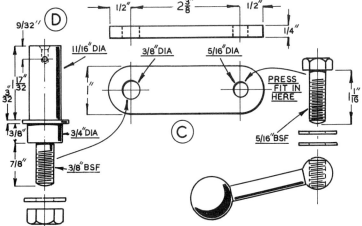

Fig. 10.10   Details of the Cowell Speed Range Device.

the correct tension for the two V-ropes transmitting the drive from the counter shaft pulley. The spindle for this pulley is depicted at 'E' in *Fig. 10.11*. This part registers in the $\frac{3}{4}''$ diameter eye of the bracket 'A' and also forms an anchorage for the jockey pulley arm 'F'. The jockey pulleys themselves run on a spindle fixed to the block 'G' which is, in turn, carried on the jockey pulley arm.

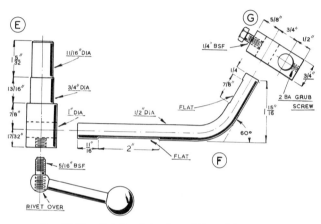

Fig. 10.11   Details of the Cowell Speed Range Device.

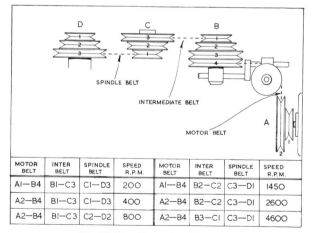

MOTOR BELT	INTER BELT	SPINDLE BELT	SPEED R.P.M.	MOTOR BELT	INTER BELT	SPINDLE BELT	SPEED R.P.M.
AI—B4	BI—C3	CI—D3	200	AI—B4	B2—C2	C3—DI	1450
A2—B4	BI—C3	CI—D3	400	A2—B4	B2—C2	C3—DI	2600
A2—B4	BI—C3	C2—D2	800	A2—B4	B3—CI	C3—DI	4600

Fig. 10.12   Champion Speed Range.

The Champion Drilling Machine Speed Range

The Champion machine was in fact the first to be modified so that an increased range of speeds could be obtained. After making the necessary alterations the range of speeds now available was as shown in *Fig. 10.12.*
The general arrangement of the device is illustrated in *Fig. 10.13.* Apart from two special pulleys and the spindles to carry them, two simple brackets need to be made. These are the brackets marked 'A' and 'B' in the drawing where their location will be clear. The V-ropes in use were obtained from stockists in London, Messrs. A. F. Mountain Ltd., 307 Borough High St., London SE.1.
The bracket 'B' is secured by the hexagon screws seen in the illustration. These are drilled and tapped 2B.A. so that allen screws passing through can be used to secure the headcasting to the drill column as depicted in *Fig. 10.14.*

Adjustable Return Spring Control

All drilling machines have some means of automatically returning the drill spindle to its upper position once the feed handle has been released. On simple machines this is effected, for the most part, by some form of spring system. Both the 'Champion' and 'Cowell' machines have a system employing a clock spring to provide the energy required. As supplied, these machines have no means of varying the spring tension. However, in neither case, is it a difficult matter to modify the machine so that the spring tension can be varied.
In *Fig. 10.15* the control system fitted by the author to a 'Champion' machine is depicted in section. This comprises a spring box 'A' fitting neatly to the tunnel in the drill head machined to accommodate the feed shaft. The cover 'B' is machined from the plastic top off a cosmetic pot. This component had nicely moulded finger grips so was most suitable for the purpose. A spigot 'C' is made a press fit in the feed shaft, the spigot having a slot cut in its outer end to accommodate the inner convolution of the spring 'D'. The outer end of the spring is finished in a loop that is passed over a pin 'E' rivetted to the inside of the spring box. It will be evident, then, that by turning the plastic cap the spring can be wound up or unwound to suit the sensitivity required for any given drill size. Though not shown in the illustration a knurled finger screw locks the spring box once the right setting has been obtained.
As a guide to the details of the components these are illustrated with dimensional information in *Fig. 10.16.*

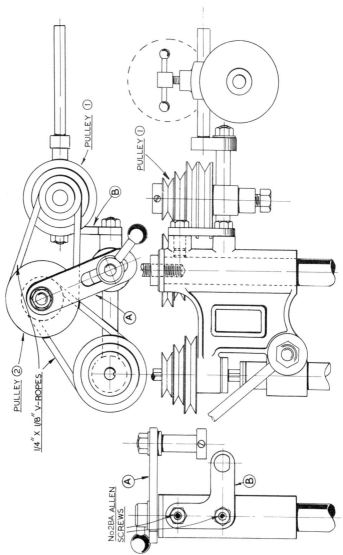

Fig. 10.13   General Arrangement of the Champion Speed Range.

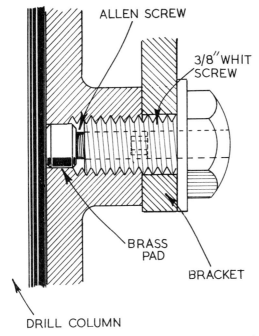

Fig. 10.14 Column Anchorage for the Speed range.

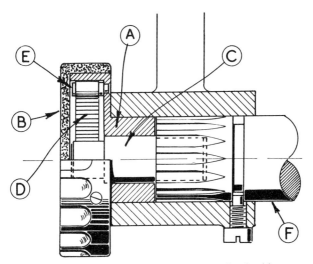

Fig. 10.15 Spring return system for champion feed lever.

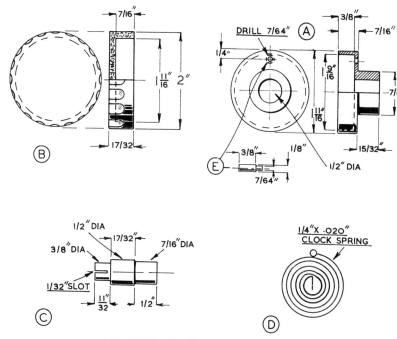

Fig. 10.16   Details of the spring return.

CHAPTER ELEVEN

CORRECT AND INCORRECT OPERATIONAL METHODS

In previous chapters certain procedures in the working of a drilling machine have been described. There are however other basic considerations that must be observed if successful drilling operations are to be the outcome of one's labours. It is the purpose of this chapter, therefore, to group together, as far as possible, many of these requirements to correct working and to present them in a series of Right and Wrong illustrations that it is hoped will help to drive home the point being made.

Mounting Drills and Chucks in the Spindle

We may as well begin with the drill itself, for without its point running accurately little success is likely to result. As we have seen earlier both chucks and drills are often supplied with taper shanks that fit directly into corresponding taper sockets machined in the drilling machine spindle itself. It follows, therefore, that the fit of the two parts must be perfect or the drill as a whole will be thrown out of alignment.

The shank for the most part, relies for its driving power on the correctness of the fit of its taper portion within the spindle. Any factor that upsets this condition will throw the drill out of line. Apart from bruising damage to the taper itself a piece of swarf wedged between the shank and the spindle, or a damaged tang, will both spoil the alignment.

These points are brought out in the illustration *Fig. 11.1*. Where a chuck is concerned it is obviously a waste of time to mount bent drills or any that have badly torn or mishapen shanks.

When inserting either chucks or taper shank drills into the spindle of a drilling machine on no account should they be hit with a hammer in order to secure them. Instead a piece of wood or soft metal should be used to support the chuck, or the drill as the case may be, and the feed lever of the machine be operated in order to

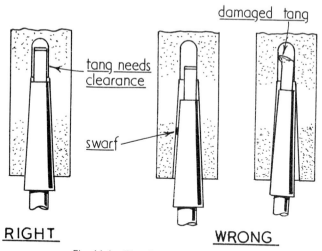

Fig. 11.1   The shanks of Morse Taper Drills.

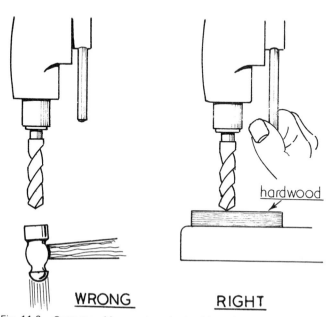

Fig. 11.2   Correct and incorrect methods of inserting taper shank drills.

apply the necessary pressure. By adopting this procedure, as illustrated in *Fig. 11.2*, no damage can possibly result, but be sure that the shanks and the bore of the spindle are oil-free or the mating surfaces will not grip each other.

Preventing damage to the worktable

Unless steps are taken to offset it the worktable can easily be damaged in a number of ways. Perhaps the most common complaint, as was demonstrated by so many drilling machines off-loaded on the surplus market after two world wars, is damage caused by the drill point breaking through the work into the table surface.

The trouble is easy to avoid if the work is supported on parallels or on two pieces of scrap metal so that when the drill point does break through it does so into fresh air. If, in addition the spindle depth stop is set so as to ensure that the point of the drill only just breaks through then all will be made doubly secure. The requirements are depicted in *Fig. 11.3*.

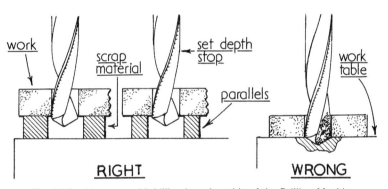

Fig. 11.3   How to avoid drilling into the table of the Drilling Machine.

A further source of damage can come from incorrectly fitted or unsuitable T-slot bolts, or from ordinary bolts used to secure work directly to the table when passed through slots in the table itself.

Bolts with heads that are too small are most likely to cause the damage depicted in *Fig. 11.4*. The smallness of the heads localises the forces acting on the slot so can easily cause the damage illustrated. The possibility can be overcome by the fitting of correctly formed T-slot nuts tapped to accept studs that can be used to secure

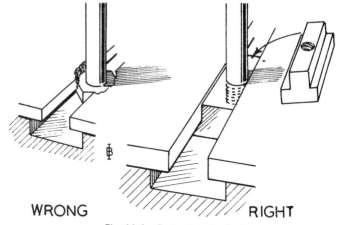

WRONG **RIGHT**

Fig. 11.4 Protecting the T-slot.

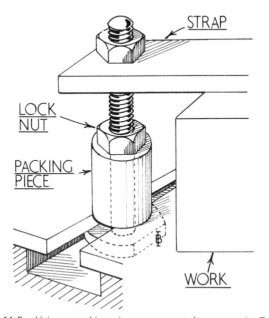

Fig. 11.5 Using a packing piece to prevent damage to the T-slot.

the work. These nuts spread the load widely so reducing the likelihood of fracture.

Machines of light construction need the further protection that can be afforded by ensuring that whatever is being secured is directly over the T-slot nut. In this way the table material is sandwiched between the work and the nut itself. If this provision cannot be ensured then it can be simulated, if that is the right word, by a pad that can be bolted down to the table surface. The upward pressure applied by bolting down the work itself is then spread evenly. The principle employed is depicted in the illustration *Fig. 11.5*.

It is particularly applicable when the work has to be held down by a series of straps.

It should be remembered that the action of drilling tends to twist the work around on the work table, and that the twisting action is very considerable when the drill in use is large. It is then advisable to bolt a pair of stops to the table and to fix them in contact with the work. The stops should, of course, be placed against opposite corners of the work in order to obtain complete security.

Cross-drilling off centre

It is sometimes necessary to cross-drill holes at right angles to another hole but not passing through its centre. If the process is attempted without adequate precaution then the result is very likely to be a broken drill as depicted in *Fig. 11.6*. The way to avoid this difficulty is to fit a plug to the work and to drill clear through the work in the way illustrated. The plug may be a mating component needing cross-pinning; in either event the two parts should be a firm fit or drill breakage will occur.

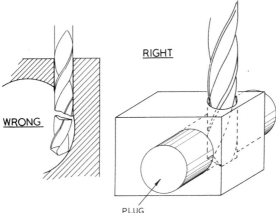

Fig. 11.6   Correct method of drilling off-centre.

Starting Holes on Round or Inclined Surfaces

It is impossible to start a hole with a drill directly on a curved or inclined surface, for the drill will wander away from any centres marked on the work. It is necessary, therefore, to provide a flat surface on which the drill can be started without it wandering off centre. There are two ways of doing this. If the curvature is small the procedure depicted in *Fig. 11.7* can be adopted. Here it is possible (A1) to mark the work with a centre punch heavily enough to allow a slocomb centre drill to be used. Following this (A2) a pilot drill is fed into the work so that (A3) a counterbore of the same diameter as the final drill can be employed (A4).

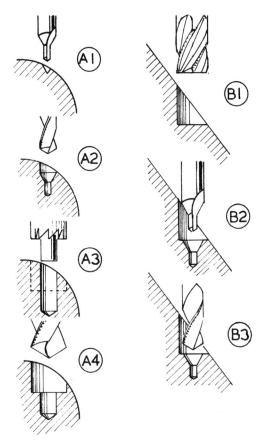

Fig. 11.7   Starting holes on round or inclined surfaces.

When the curvature is severe, or the surface is at an acute angle, then the method or sequence of operations outlined at 'B' in *Fig. 11.7*, has to be employed. It is again essential to provide a flat surface for successful drilling and this requirement is best achieved by an end-milling operation (B1) though this may not be possible in the drilling machine itself unless the spindle bearings are capable of withstanding the side loading the operation imposes on them, and the machine has a compound table as illustrated in *Fig. 11.8*. Once the flat surface has been produced the work can be marked off, centre drilled (B2) and finally drilled to size (B3).

Fig. 11.8   Compound table for the drilling machine

Recovery of mis-drilled holes

If, after marking off, the resulting hole is found to be off-centre all may not be lost provided certain steps are carried out. The procedure to be described necessarily applies to holes drilled clear through the work. The illustration *Fig. 11.9* depicts the sequence of events. In this diagram the sequence (1) shows what occurs when a hole is drilled correctly, while at (2) the drilled hole is seen to wander off-centre on being opened up. It is then that by the use of a hand file, the hole is re-centred. After this it is opened out to size by drilling.

The Machine Vice

One might be forgiven for thinking that no comment about the machine vice is needed, but from time to time the author has seen certain malpractices adopted in connection with the mounting of the vice itself or the work that is to be placed in it, so a few words on the subject would seem justified.

In the first place the vice must be placed on a clean work table and not on top of small pieces of swarf that might throw the vice's alignment out of true. See *Fig. 11.10 (1)*. The same remarks apply to the work itself when placed in the jaws of the vice. As the result of previous machining operations the work may develop burrs which, if not removed, would cause the work to be propped up out of true (2). Additionally, if the burring came into contact with the vice jaws the work could be insecurely held (2). Care must also be taken to see the jaws are clean and that no swarf is left on the bed of the vice or the work will be set out of truth (3).

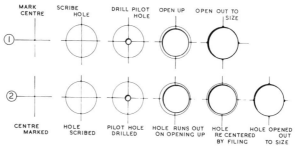

Fig. 11.9   Recovery of mis-drilled holes.

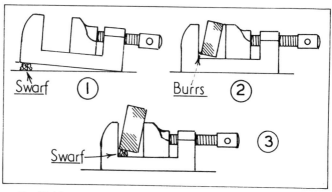

Fig. 11.10   Correct and incorrect methods when using the vice.

CHAPTER TWELVE

ELECTRIC HAND DRILLS

For many years now electric hand drills have been available to industry but it is only comparatively recently that they have come into general use amongst amateurs and those members of the public who like 'Do-it-Yourself' operations.

It is manifestly impossible to describe all the various makes that are available. Instead, some typical tools will form the basis for this chapter, together with fitments that can be used with them in the context of drilling.

The Black & Decker D820 Drill

Amongst the many machines on the market the Black & Decker series of drills have long been popular. The author numbers one of

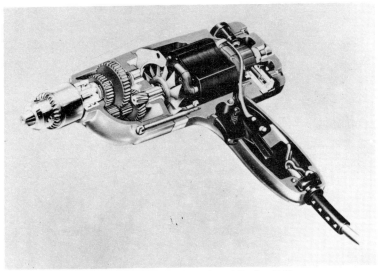

Fig. 12.1   Section of Black and Decker Drill.

139

these amongst the equipment in his workshop and it has proved itself to be most reliable after several years use. The machine in question is the D820 drill. It has two speeds 900 r.p.m. and 2400 r.p.m. and is suppressed so that it will not cause interference on television. Its drilling capacities are:—

In steel—$\frac{3}{8}''$.
In masonry—$\frac{1}{2}''$.
In hard wood—$\frac{3}{4}''$.

Whilst in the case of hole saws that will be mentioned later the maximum size that can be used is $1\frac{1}{2}''$ diameter.

In common with other makes the Black & Decker drills have pistol grip handles housing the motor switch, and a second hand hold that can be attached to either side of the machine to accommodate left- or right-handed users. The drill has frictionless bearings and sealed-in lubrication.

The Wolf Safetymaster Drills

An example of this range of machines is illustrated in *Fig. 12.2.* This is a $\frac{1}{4}''$ capacity drill type SM2 with two speeds available. These are selected by a sliding control located on the upper side of the machine just behind the gearbox itself. The speeds available on a 'no load' basis are:—

High Speed 3700 r.p.m. approximately.
Low Speed 1800 r.p.m. approximately.

The drill is 'double insulated'. This means that, as the makers claim, it need not be earthed as is essential with other types of machine. This is a matter we shall return to later.

Additional Speed Increasing and Reducing Devices

The speeds obtainable with most electric hand drills are too high for many purposes. For example the drilling of masonry and hard wood needs a considerable reduction in operating speeds. The Rawlplug Company have provided a simple solution to the problem in the De-Speeder equipment manufactured by them. These devices are self-contained units that need only to be gripped in the chuck of the hand drill and do not involve any removal of parts from the drill itself. There are five types of De-Speeder available, the first three have a 4 to 1 speed reduction with fitted chucks of 5/16, 3/8 and 1/2 inch capacity respectively. The fourth is a 2-speed device with speed reductions of 3 to 1 and 9 to 1 whilst the fifth type is a

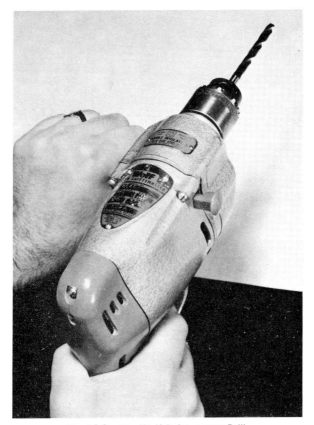

Fig. 12.2 The Wolf Safetymaster Drill.

reversing model having a forward speed reduction of 12 to 1 and a speed reduction of 4 to 1 in reverse. The method of mounting the device in an electric drill is depicted in *Fig. 12.3*.

The De-Speeder is in effect an epicyclic gearbox whose input shaft is gripped in the chuck of the hand drill whilst the output shaft of the fitment accommodates a chuck in which the actual drill to be used is fitted. The third element in any simple epicyclic gear system is the arcular or ring gear that surrounds it. When this gear can turn freely the output shaft will not rotate. If, on the other hand, a constraint is placed on the ring gears movement then the output shaft will start to revolve. In the De-Speeder the ring gear is anchored, to or forms part of the casing. In use, therefore, once the casing surrounding the gear system is held stationary in the hand the drill itself will revolve.

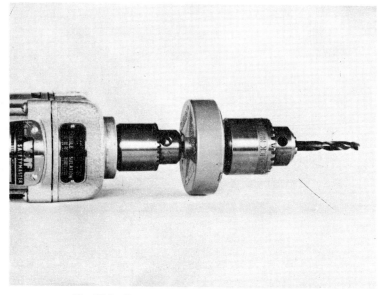

Fig. 12.3   The de-Speeder mounted in a hand drill.

A typical epicyclic gear arrangement has already been illustrated in Chapter 8.

Black & Decker market a speed-changing device that can be instantly fitted to the hand drill. This is a right-angled fitment that can be used either to reduce speed or, if reversed in the chuck, to increase it. The ratio of the gears is 2 to 1 so the speeds can either be halved or doubled.

Mounting the Drill

Both firms whose products have been mentioned provide stands enabling the drill to be mounted so converting the assembly into a complete drilling machine. The Black & Decker stand is illustrated in *Fig. 12.4*. The drill is held in a bracket that slides on the column and is controlled by a hand lever. The position of the drill is adjustable both radially and vertically, but no angular setting is available. On the other hand the drill stand made by Wolf can be adjusted to enable work to be drilled at an angle. The stand itself is depicted in *Fig. 12.5*, where the lever used to lock the column after the angle has been adjusted is seen to the left at the bottom of the picture. The electric drill depicted in the illustration is the Wolf

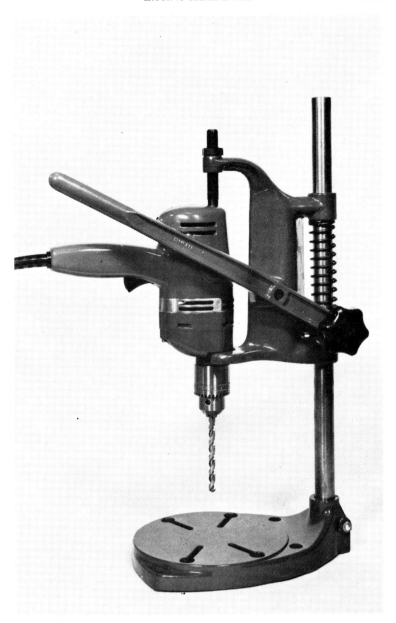

Fig. 12.4   The Black and Decker Stand.

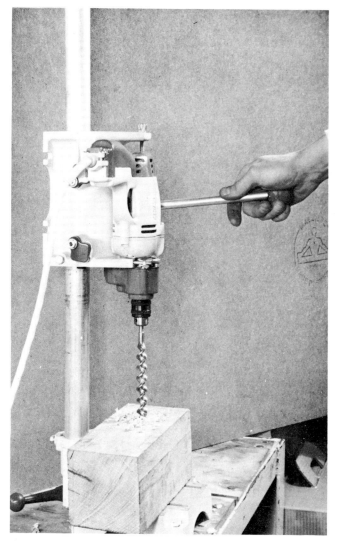

Fig. 12.5   The Wolf Drill Stand.

'Safetymaster' fitted with a 'Lo-speed' Reducer enabling a drill of $\frac{7}{8}''$ diameter to be used in oak.

Drills and Cutters

As has been said earlier the electric hand drill is largely used by the amateur for work about the house or in connection with woodwork in one form or the other. Much of the drilling involved is free hand, punching holes in masonry so that cabinets, shelves and the like can be secured. For this purpose twist drills normally employed for the drilling of metal will not serve because the abrasive qualities of masonry soon ruins them. Instead drills tipped with tungsten carbide need to be used. Tungsten Carbide is a very hard substance used in the machine shop in connection with the turning of tough material. Commercially, these special drills bear a brand name such as 'Durium' and the like. They must be run at a low speed or even their keen edge will vanish. A typical drill is depicted in *Fig. 12.6* at 'A'

Wood-Working Twist Drills

Standard twist drills serve well for holes up to $\frac{1}{4}''$ diameter. Holes above this size specially modified twist drills are obtainable. An example is depicted in the illustration *Fig. 12.6*.

The drill illustrated in *Fig. 12.6* at 'B' is a product of the Sheffield Twist Drill Company and marketed under the brand name 'Dormer'. It is ground to the form depicted, having a spear point that can be used to engage centres marked on the work when they exist, and the cutting lips set at an angle so that initially they cut at their outer

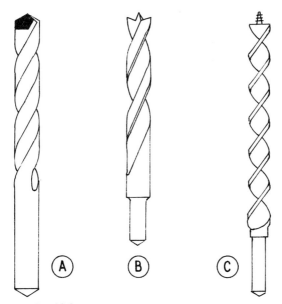

Fig. 12.6   Drills for use in the electric hand drill.

edges only. In this way the wood fibres are sheared before the lips themselves remove the bulk material. These drills cut a clean hole but, of course, need a backing under the work to avoid tearing at the breakthrough of the drill itself.

The sizes obtainable are $\frac{1}{4}''$, $\frac{5}{16}''$, $\frac{3}{8}''$, $\frac{7}{16}''$ and $\frac{1}{2}''$ diameter all having a $\frac{1}{4}''$ diameter spigot machined on the shank to enable them to be used in the smaller electric hand drills.

Augur Bit

For diameters above $\frac{1}{2}''$ the augur bit illustrated in *Fig. 12.6* 'C' is commonly employed. This tool is available in diameters from $\frac{3}{8}''$ to $2''$. The centre point is furnished with a helical scroll similar to that found on woodscrews. The object of the scroll is to assist in feeding the augur into the workpiece. Whilst this may be an advantage when using the larger sizes of augur, it is definitely a dangerous provision when applied to the smaller diameters of the bit. Unless care is taken the scroll tends to take charge and wind the augur into the work at a rate that may well prove dangerous, if not impossible to control.

APPENDIX

COMBINATION CENTRE DRILLS

Size	Diam. of body in.	Diam. of drill in.	Size	Diam. of body in.	Diam. of drill in.
A	3/10	3/32–1/8	1	1/2	7/32
B	3/10	1/8	2	1/2	9/32
C	3/10	3/32	3	1/2	11/32
D	15/64	5/64	4	1/2	13/32
E	13/64	1/16	5	5/8	7/32
F.1	7/16	5/32	6	5/8	9/32
F.2	7/16	3/16	7	5/8	11/32
H	5/32	3/64	8	5/8	13/32
L	13/64	1/16–No. 45	9	3/4	1/4
R	7/16	5/32–3/16	10	3/4	5/16
S	1/8	No. 57			

BRITISH STANDARD CENTRE DRILLS

Size	Diam. of body in.	Diam. of drill in.	Size	Diam. of body in.	Diam. of drill in.
B.S.1	1/8	3/64	B.S.5	7/16	3/16
B.S.2	3/16	1/16	B.S.6	5/8	1/4
B.S.3	1/4	3/32	B.S.7	3/4	5/16
B.S.4	5/16	1/8			

TWIST DRILLS

Inch or gauge	*m/m*	*Decimal Inch*	*Inch or gauge*	*m/m*	*Decimal Inch*
80		.0135	66		.0330
	.35	.0138		.85	.0335
79		.0145		.875	.0344
	.375	.0148	65		.0350
1/64		.0156		.9	.0354
	.4	.0157	64		.0360
78		.0160		.925	.0364
	.425	.0167	63		.0370
	.45	.0177		.95	.0374
77		.0180	62		.0380
	.475	.0187		.975	.0384
	.5	.0197	61		.0390
76		.0200		1.00	.0394
	.525	.0207	60		.0400
75		.0210	59		.0410
	.55	.0216		1.05	.0413
74		.0225	58		.0420
	.575	.0226	57		.0430
	.6	.0236		1.1	.0433
73		.0240		1.15	.0453
	.625	.0246	56		.0465
72		.0250	3/64		.0469
	.65	.0256		1.2	.0472
71		.0260		1.25	.0492
	.675	.0266		1.3	.0512
	.7	.0276	55		.0520
70		.0280		1.35	.0531
	.725	.0285	54		.0550
69		.0292		1.4	.0551
	.75	.0295		1.45	.0571
	.775	.0305		1.5	.0590
68		.0310	53		.0595
1/32		.0312		1.55	.0610
	.8	.0315	1/16		.0625
67		.0320		1.6	.0630
	.825	.0325			

Inch or gauge	m/m	Decimal Inch	Inch or gauge	m/m	Decimal Inch
52		.0635	37		.1040
	1.65	.0650		2.65	.1043
	1.7	.0669		2.7	.1063
51		.0670	36		.1065
	1.75	.0689		2.75	.1083
50		.0700	7/64		.1094
	1.8	.0709	35		.1100
	1.85	.0728		2.8	.1102
49		.0730	34		.1110
	1.9	.0748		2.85	.1122
48		.0760	33		.1130
	1.95	.0768		2.9	.1142
5/64		.0781	32		.1160
47		.0785		2.95	.1161
	2.00	.0787		3.00	.1181
	2.05	.0807	31		.1200
46		.0810		3.05	.1201
45		.0820		3.1	.1220
	2.1	.0827		3.15	.1240
	2.15	.0846	1/8		.1250
44		.0860		3.2	.1260
	2.2	.0866		3.25	.1280
	2.25	.0886	30		.1285
43		.0890		3.3	.1299
	2.3	.0906		3.35	.1319
	2.35	.0925		3.4	.1339
42		.0935		3.45	.1358
3/32		.0938	29		.1360
	2.4	.0945		3.5	.1378
41		.0960		3.55	.1398
	2.45	.0964	28		.1405
40		.0980	9/64		.1406
	2.5	.0984		3.6	.1417
39		.0995		3.65	.1437
	2.55	.1004	27		.1440
38		.1015		3.7	.1457
	2.6	.1024	26		.1470
				3.75	.1476

Inch or gauge	m/m	Decimal Inch	Inch or gauge	m/m	Decimal Inch
25		.1495	11		.1910
	3.8	.1496		4.9	.1929
	3.85	.1516	10		.1935
24		.1520		4.95	.1949
	3.9	.1535	9		.1960
23		.1540		5.00	.1968
	3.95	.1555	8		.1990
5/32		.1562		5.1	.2008
22		.1570	7		.2010
	4.00	.1575	13/64		.2031
21		.1590	6		.2040
	4.05	.1594		5.2	.2047
20		.1610	5		.2055
	4.1	.1614		5.25	.2067
	4.15	.1634		5.3	.2087
	4.2	.1654	4		.2090
19		.1660		5.4	.2126
	4.25	.1673	3		.2130
	4.3	.1693		5.5	.2165
18		.1695	7/32		.2188
	4.35	.1713		5.6	.2205
11/64		.1719	2		.2210
17		.1730		5.7	.2244
	4.4	.1732		5.75	.2264
	4.45	.1752	1		.2280
16		.1770		5.8	.2283
	4.5	.1772		5.9	.2323
	4.55	.1791	A		.2340
15		.1800	15/64		.2344
	4.6	.1811		6.00	.2362
14		.1820	B		.2380
	4.65	.1831		6.1	.2402
13	4.7	.1850	C		.2420
	4.75	.1870		6.2	.2441
3/16		.1875	D		.2460
12	4.8	.1890		6.25	.2461
	4.85	.1909		6.3	.2480

Inch or gauge	m/m	Decimal Inch	Inch or gauge	m/m	Decimal Inch
E. 1/4		.2500	P		.3230
	6.4	.2520		8.25	.3248
	6.5	.2559		8.3	.3268
F		.2570	21/64		.3281
	6.6	.2598		8.4	.3307
G		.2610	Q		.3320
	6.7	.2638		8.5	.3346
17/64		.2656		8.6	.3386
	6.75	.2657	R		.3390
H		.2660		8.7	.3425
	6.8	.2677	11/32		.3438
	6.9	.2716		8.75	.3445
I		.2720		8.8	.3465
	7.00	.2756	S		.3480
J		.2770		8.9	.3504
	7.1	.2795		9.00	.3543
K		.2810	T		.3580
9/32		.2812		9.1	.3583
	7.2	.2835	23/64		.3594
	7.25	.2854		9.2	.3622
	7.3	.2874		9.25	.3642
L		.2900		9.3	.3661
	7.4	.2913	U		.3680
M		.2950		9.4	.3701
	7.5	.2953		9.5	.3740
19/64		.2969	3/8		.3750
	7.6	.2992	V		.3770
N		.3020		9.6	.3780
	7.7	.3031		9.7	.3819
	7.75	.3051		9.75	.3839
	7.8	.3071		9.8	.3858
	7.9	.3110	W		.3860
5/16		.3125		9.9	.3898
	8.00	.3150	25/64		.3906
O		.3160		10.00	.3937
	8.1	.3189	X		.3970
	8.2	.3228		10.1	.3976
				10.2	.4016
				10.25	.4035

Inch or gauge	m/m	Decimal Inch	Inch or gauge	m/m	Decimal Inch
Y		.4040	1/2	12.7	.5000
	10.3	.4055		12.75	.5020
13/32		.4062		12.8	.5039
	10.4	.4094		12.9	.5079
Z		.4130		13.00	.5118
	10.5	.4134	33/64		.5156
	10.6	.4173		13.25	.5216
	10.7	.4213	17/32		.5312
27/64		.4219		13.5	.5315
	10.75	.4232		13.75	.5413
	10.8	.4252	35/64		.5469
	10.9	.4291		14.00	.5512
	11.00	.4331		14.25	.5610
	11.1	.4370	9/16		.5625
7/16		.4375		14.5	.5709
	11.2	.4409	37/64		.5781
	11.25	.4429		14.75	.5807
	11.3	.4449		15.00	.5906
	11.4	.4488	19/32		.5938
	11.5	.4528		15.25	.6004
29/64		.4531	39/64		.6094
	11.6	.4567		15.5	.6102
	11.7	.4606		15.75	.6201
	11.75	.4626	5/8		.6250
	11.8	.4646		16.00	.6299
	11.9	.4685		16.25	.6398
15/32		.4688	41/64		.6406
	12.00	.4724		16.5	.6496
	12.1	.4764	21/32		.6562
	12.2	.4803		16.75	.6594
	12.25	.4823		17.00	.6693
	12.3	.4842	43/64		.6719
31/64		.4844		17.25	.6791
	12.4	.4882	11/16		.6875
	12.5	.4921		17.5	.6890
	12.6	.4961		17.75	.6988

Inch	m/m	Decimal Inch	Inch	m/m	Decimal Inch
45/64		.7031	59/64		.9219
	18.00	.7087		23.5	.9252
	18.25	.7185		23.75	.9350
23/32		.7188	15/16		.9375
	18.5	.7284		24.00	.9449
47/64		.7344	61/64		.9531
	18.75	.7382		24.25	.9547
	19.00	.7480		24.5	.9646
3/4		.7500	31/32		.9688
	19.25	.7579		24.75	.9744
49/64		.7656		25.00	.9842
	19.5	.7677	63/64		.9844
	19.75	.7776	1		1.0000
25/32		.7812			
	20.00	.7874			
51/64		.7969			
	20.25	.7972			
	20.5	.8071			
13/16		.8125			
	20.75	.8169			
	21.00	.8268			
53/64		.8281			
	21.25	.8366			
27/32		.8438			
	21.5	.8465			
	2.751	.8563			
55/64		.8594			
	22.00	.8661			
7/8		.8750			
	22.25	.8760			
	22.5	.8858			
57/64		.8906			
	22.75	.8957			
	23.00	.9055			
29/32		.9062			
	23.25	.9154			

INDEX

Index